No Fighting,
No Biting,
No Screaming

of related interest

Practical Behaviour Management Solutions for Children and Teens with Autism
The 5P Approach
Linda Miller
ISBN 978 1 84905 038 8

People with Autism Behaving Badly
Helping People with ASD Move On from Behavioral and Emotional Challenges
John Clements
ISBN 978 1 84310 765 1

Managing Family Meltdown
The Low Arousal Approach and Autism
Linda Woodcock and Andrea Page
Foreword by Andrew McDonnell
ISBN 978 1 84905 009 8

Bo Hejlskov Elvén

No Fighting, No Biting, No Screaming

How to Make Behaving Positively Possible for People with Autism and Other Developmental Disabilities

Jessica Kingsley *Publishers*
London and Philadelphia

First published in 2010
by Jessica Kingsley Publishers
116 Pentonville Road
London N1 9JB, UK
and
400 Market Street, Suite 400
Philadelphia, PA 19106, USA
www.jkp.com

Copyright © Bo Hejlskov Elvén 2010
Translated from Swedish by Teresa Elvén

Library of Congress Cataloging in Publication Data
A CIP catalog record for this book is available from the Library of Congress

British Library Cataloguing in Publication Data
A CIP catalogue record for this book is available from the British Library

ISBN 978 1 84905 126 2

Printed and bound in the United States by
Thomson-Shore, 7300 Joy Road, Dexter, MI 48130

Christer Magnusson and

Angellika Arndt

d.2006

• • • • •

Contents

Introduction

Challenging behaviour is often regarded as certain specific behaviours. These might be hitting, biting, kicking, screaming or any other kind of behaviour that feels offensive to staff or parents. There are many books on the market about how to change these behaviours, often using cognitive behavioural methods. This is not that kind of book. What you have just started reading is a book on how to understand and manage challenging behaviour in a person with developmental disabilities in order to make daily life a good life.

Parents of children with developmental disabilities often tell me that on becoming parents they started out practising more or less the same methods their own parents used rearing and disciplining them; but that after a while they realized that these did not work as intended. Frequently they would then double their efforts, using the same methods. When they finally realized that their methods would not work at all, in many cases they would start wondering if there was something wrong with their child, and even contact a child psychiatric service, the school psychologist or the family doctor for an assessment. In some cases this resulted in a diagnosis.

Getting a diagnosis is often considered the point of change. The parents' suspicion that the problem lies with the child and not the fostering methods is confirmed. The problem is that after assessment, the doctors and psychologists don't return the child with a managing manual. Often the parents continue using exactly the same fostering methods that made them contact the doctors and psychologists in the first place. And obviously enough, they still don't work. The child still says no to everything the parents suggest, she still fights, bites, throws toys and screams. And after a while the parents' relief at having got an explanation for the child's behaviour vanishes. The feeling of powerlessness is back.

The intention of this book is to be a managing manual for parents dealing with behaviour that makes them wonder whether their methods are poor or whether there is something wrong with their child. It is also intended to be a managing manual for staff working with people with developmental disabilities. The problems of the two groups are similar: the fostering methods used by our own parents don't work, but few of us have learned different methods. That is the reason this book is not only a book on theory; it is also a book on hands-on methods that encourage positive behaviour, while also giving advice on how to manage challenging behaviour. In the book we will look at methods that make people say yes to our suggestions as well as methods for avoiding conflicts. All in order to make you as parents or members of staff feel able and successful, but most of all to create possibilities for a good life for people with developmental disabilities.

I intend to help the reader understand and relate to the difficulties experienced by members of staff or parents of children with the neuropsychiatric disorders autism, attention-deficit hyperactivity disorder (ADHD), Asperger's syndrome or Tourette's syndrome. But I don't want to limit myself to that. I believe that the same kind of thinking can be used working with people with Down's syndrome or intellectual disabilities. This may sound a wide and ambitious goal given that these separate diagnoses seem very different, but the associated behavioural disorders are often very similar.

The book isn't limited to children either, but deals with how to handle challenging behaviour in all people with the diagnoses above. Therefore this isn't just a book for parents, but also for people working in care settings, rehabilitation, schools and, to a certain extent, to the psychiatric discipline.

For this reason I have chosen to call the main characters service-users. They can be children, pupils, clients, patients, partakers or citizens in different contexts, but to me it has been important to find a term that doesn't reveal age or relationship with the person. Service-user covers everybody who is offered special educational assistance, but I acknowledge is not the most apt term for a child with ADHD at home in his or her family. I have chosen it because it is a term that offers the person in question more to say than client or pupil, but still focuses on who is the object of the effort. The staff are there for the service-user, not the other way round.

This book is not intended to be a psychological text book or a scientific dissertation. Therefore there are few notes on further reading and scientific argumentation. In cases when I do refer to direct scientific studies, I have given them as footnotes in order not to disturb the reader. I am a practitioner and work with people with challenging behaviour, which characterizes the book, so theories and available research are used where it renders meaning to the practical work. My work is founded on a view of people that is based on psychological and philosophical theory, which I have tried to account for where needed.

The methods described here are complex and require adaptation to specific situations and service-users. Therefore it can be difficult to measure what works and what doesn't. It is not an uncommon problem in special education activities. The reason for this is that people with the problems this book discusses are very different. The difference between a person with Asperger's syndrome and a person with intellectual disability and autism is huge, even though both have an autism spectrum disorder (ASD). One of them may have a job as an engineer and the other lack language, live in a supervised group home and have daily life therapy. The methods I will describe have a theoretical background as well as being based on experience and evidence. They have primarily been developed in England and are, among others, documented in Andy McDonnell's research.[*]

The book is driven by theory, research and real examples. Almost all examples are from my clinical work and concern real people and their problems and difficulties to function in daily life. All names and other identifying details have been changed, except for those who have given permission for their names to be used.

The book begins with the main traits of challenging behaviour and a discussion on fundamental views of humankind. In Chapter two I consider what preconceptions parents and staff sometimes have about working with challenging behaviour and about what should

---

[*]   McDonnell 2010

guide our behaviour in daily life with people with developmental disabilities. Chapter three deals with methods of managing challenging behaviour, where adjustment of demands, affective methods and diversion are dealt with in a concrete and easily accessible way. Chapter four deals with how to relate to the causes of the behaviour as well as discussing how it is possible to work from a psychological point of view of stress to avoid the arousal of challenging behaviour. Chapter five then looks at methods we can use to deal with conflict when it arises and calm situations down. Finally, the book ends with a summary and a hope for the future in chapter six.

Unfortunately, I can't take credit for all the thoughts put forward in this book. Some of them have been thought out by others – from Søren Kierkegaard to Aaron Antonovsky, Andy McDonnell and Ross W. Greene. The stress model in chapter four has been developed in cooperation with Trine Uhrskov, and many thoughts have matured in discussions with my colleagues, among whom Hanne Veje with her practical approach and smooth intellect has been of considerable help. All thoughts and methods of course have been verified by exchanges of experience with my colleagues and all the people I have guided throughout the years. I am unfathomably indebted to all these people for the work they do for people with different difficulties and for the difference they make in people's lives. Thank you.

I would also like to thank Åsa Nilsonne for her encouragement to write this book, Sophie Dow, Leif Grieffelde and Tord Jerfsten for their opinions on the manuscript and Teresa Elvén for invaluable and necessary linguistic help.

Chapter 1
· · · · · · ·
Challenging Behaviour: Definitions and Theories

What is challenging behaviour?

Challenging behaviour is often regarded as given types of behaviour. In legislation certain types of behaviour are allowed whereas others, for example stealing and fighting, are not. When I hold courses on managing challenging behaviour, I am often given examples that indicate coherence with what is intended in educational or care contexts. These can be disobedience, refusals, screaming, conflict behaviour, hitting, kicking, biting, running away, biting one's hand or slamming one's head on the floor. However, we all know that certain behaviour can be OK in one context but challenging in another.

> **Lee** is 14 years old and is in eighth grade. He is in town one Wednesday afternoon. A slightly older boy approaches him and says: 'Give me your mobile or you'll get a beating.' Lee refuses, whereupon the boy starts beating him. Lee hits back, the boy is surprised and falls, and Lee runs away.

Lee does something that in other contexts would be considered challenging behaviour. However, everybody understands that he is defending himself, and he would never be charged with physical abuse even though he has hit the older boy. This means that it is not the behaviour alone that defines whether it is challenging or not, but also its context.

Contexts are important for how we manage and understand behaviour, and this is true for educational and care activities as well. Behaviour that we accept from a service-user with intellectual disability and autism, we would not readily accept in mainstream schools. Besides, there is an aspect of educational and care work we can't forget: the staff are paid to provide care for the service-users, which means that the responsibility for the behaviour and its contexts lies with the staff. If you have responsibility for behaviour management, you must of course learn its methods.

There has always been behaviour that has been defined as challenging. The behaviours have been described differently throughout the years, and rules, laws and legal systems have been created in order to manage them in society. The reason has been that people survive best in groups, and if we are to be in a group we must be able to assume social behaviours. Consequently, we have developed abilities that help us in this, like a manifest docility; we would rather say yes than no, and in order to take part in social contexts we are open to compromises.

Norms of behaviour often have solidarity as the point of departure. The Ten Commandments is a good example of that. They regularize the contact between children and parents, and between neighbours in a small community, they deal with rights to property, and so on, and put these in a religious context so there is a reason to follow them. The laws and norms of today are not far from the Ten Commandments, but are more complex to fit a more complex society.

There have always been people who haven't been able to follow the rules and norms of society. Among these are society's 'misfits'. We don't know how this was handled a long time ago, but we know that by the development of European society, we began to place these people separately as they could not follow our common rules. Until 1801, people with behavioural disorders or other deviations were placed in so-called asylums, no matter whether in respect of criminal behaviour, intellectual disability, dementia or schizophrenia. In 1801 they began to separate criminal individuals from the others (chief physician Pinel at La Salpêtrière in Paris made a difference between what is commonly called 'the bad' and 'the mad'), and not until about 100 years later was a separation between the mentally ill and people with intellectual disability carried out. However, these groups were still kept secluded from society until the discontinuation of the mental hospitals and the central institutions for people with intellectual disabilities in the 1980s.

Then of course we also have all those who don't follow rules and norms, but don't have a diagnosis and whose behaviour is not serious enough to be considered criminal. We have always been able to regularize such people with different fostering methods.

Our image of challenging behaviour is often based on knowledge of relatively well-functioning people. Ever since the 17th and 18th centuries, and the philosophers Descartes, Spinoza and Kant, we have considered behaviour to be something that is chosen actively and rationally, which renders punishment a logical consequence. This image means that our methods often spring from the idea that behaviour is something rational and deliberate, and that you therefore can make people choose differently if the consequence of the behaviour is made clear, or if you through punishment and scolding make sure the challenging behaviour becomes a problem to the person with the behaviour.

This is clearly not always the case. Often when behaviour is considered challenging to staff or parents, it is not obvious to whom it actually is a problem. Emerson's acknowledged research definition of challenging behaviour is:

> Culturally abnormal behaviour of such an intensity, frequency or durance that the physical safety of the person itself or that of others is likely to be put at a risk, or behaviour that probably greatly limits the person in the use of, or results in the person being denied access to, common physical public places or services.[*]

This is a quite complicated and difficult definition to master. It doesn't deal with what the behaviour may be, but with the consequences of the behaviour for the person who has it. On the other hand, I think this is better than only defining certain types of behaviour,

---

[*]   Emerson 2001, p.3.

but it is not good enough. I believe that what defines the behaviour more than anything is that it makes other people feel inadequate and powerless.

> **Charlotte** is 16 years old and has autism. When she is feeling anxious or restless she hurts herself, especially in the head. Sometimes she bleeds severely from wounds on her cheek.

> **Nicholas** is 32 years old. He has severe intellectual disability. He likes strong smells and when he is bored he puts his index finger in his trousers and gets some poo that he smears under his nose. Then he breathes in heavily and is unmistakably happy.

> **Saleem** is 19 years old and has autism. He has realized that he is sent to his room every time he takes his pants off. Therefore he has developed a type of behaviour: he takes off his trousers whenever he wants to go home. This happens in town, in the woods, at the doctor's, etc.

> **Mikey** is ten years old and has ADHD. His activity level is very high and he normally runs around in the corridors at school. The teachers have told him not to ever since he started school, but it hasn't had any effect.

> **Agnes** is 12 years old and has severe intellectual disability. Furthermore she is tied to a wheelchair. She is a happy girl who doesn't hurt herself or anyone else. The staff at school ask for guidance because Agnes claps her hands all day, which is difficult for the personnel to endure.

What these types of behaviour have in common is that they are hard to change. The staff feel powerless as they can't change the behaviour, and the behaviour is also hard for them to see and endure. In other words, the behaviour causes the staff problems.

My British colleague Andy McDonnell, who has developed the Studio-III method, has his own definition: challenging behaviour is behaviour that 'pisses you off'. He focuses on the feelings of the staff.

My definition, and the one we will use in this book, is:

Challenging behaviour is behaviour that causes problems for people around the person.

Nobody with intellectual disability, autism, ADHD or other developmental difficulties is referred to diagnostic assessment or treatment because they experience problems themselves. However, often we think and believe that they do. The actual reason for assessment, however, is that someone close to the person has difficulties handling and relating to the person in question. Often it turns out that the methods we use for other people don't work. We are frustrated and arrange for someone with special knowledge in behaviour, either a psychologist or psychiatrist, to take on the person in question and find out what is wrong.

I believe that it simply is the lack of power of people around the person that defines the behaviour as problematic, which means that:

- If we place the responsibility for the problem with the person with the behaviour, we have let this person down. This is done by advocating methods designed to make the person change his or her behaviour from the point of view that 'you just don't do that'. The responsibility can also be placed with the service-user by using words like demanding, refusing, oppositional, unmotivated or stubborn about him or her. The responsibility must be laid with the people around the person who are experiencing the behaviour as problematic, because they are the ones who can instigate change through their own behaviours.

- Responsibility must be placed with the person who experiences the problem if the situation is to be changed. Responsibility entails power and possibilities. To place responsibility outside oneself only reinforces the feeling of loss of power. As parents or members of staff, we must realize that we are the ones experiencing a problem, not the person with the behaviour.

- Responsibility must, if possible, be placed with someone who is motivated to change the behaviour. The motivating factor can be that we find the behaviour hard to live with, but also that we are getting paid. To place responsibility for the problem with the service-user generally means that the motivation to solve it is lacking, and then we have to accept the problem and live with it. If responsibility is placed with the professional person, the probability of the problems disappearing improves greatly.

- We must find methods that allow us to endure the behaviour and so prevent us from reacting forcefully on a behaviour that we don't approve of. If we react strongly, this affects the behaviour, but rarely in a positive way.

- If the behaviour is dangerous, we must find methods to change it. If it is not dangerous, we must form an opinion of whether it is a behaviour that is OK, even if we find it difficult. Our own feelings can't be decisive as to whether a behaviour is acceptable if it benefits the service-user.

Dangerous behaviour? Or just difficult?

Certain types of behaviour are dangerous either to *oneself* or to somebody else. Such behaviour we must deal with at once. Dangerous behaviour can be:

- hitting
- kicking
- biting
- slamming one's head into a wall
- cutting other people or oneself deeply.

However, there are many other types of behaviour that we react to because we find them difficult, but which in effect are not dangerous. This means that we may not need to deal with them at once, but that we can plan a strategy to change them. These can be:

- disobedience
- jeering
- biting one's hand
- cutting one's arm.

Disobedience is not dangerous in itself, but often renders parents and staff powerless. If you react directly and forcefully there is a risk that the conflict grows. Therefore it is often an advantage to work with disobedience on a long-term basis instead of dealing with it at once.

Jeering has its own logic. How often have we not ourselves said something we don't mean to somebody we care about? We taunt people to get an effect, an answer back. People with intellectual disabilities or neuropsychiatric disorders do exactly like we do, but have two problems in this area:

- The words don't have the same magical meaning as they have for other people. Many people find it physically hard to say for example 'I just want to die', because they feel that it may come true. In the same way most people don't use strong words like whore or four-letter words about other people. Doing so is however rarely a problem to people with intellectual disabilities or neuropsychiatric disorders.

- The effect of the words can be hard to see. If the person has difficulties reading other people's facial and emotional expressions, he or she must by necessity use a stronger word.

Therefore words that are much stronger than other people's jeers are used. Besides, these words are being used to prompt a reaction. If the desired effect is prompted, it is a success; that word becomes a good word that fills a function, and it will be used again. If parents and staff react to a forceful word by, for example, punishment, consequence or conflict, the word is strengthened. Then we can be absolutely certain that it will be used again. If we on the other hand tolerate the word, we may manage to eliminate the use of it. And that is definitely not dangerous.

The story of Christer Magnusson is violent. He died from physical restraint in his room in Uppsala in Sweden in 2006 because staff at his group home could not handle his biting his hand. Sometimes people with intellectual disability or autism bite their hand if they are in a difficult situation. The reason for biting one's hand is that it makes the person manage the situation. It is a good way to focus one's attention and is not actually dangerous. As far as I know, nobody has died from biting his or her hand, but many people have died because they, like Christer, were not allowed to. Something that was a strategy to manage a difficult situation in Christer's world was a problem to the staff.

Self-injuring behaviour of different kinds may have this background, and if the possibility to use such a strategy is removed, it is unfortunately not certain that the person has another strategy. Then there is a great risk that the person doesn't do as well, or that the person develops other types of behaviour that may well be worse.

> **Jessica** was ten years old when she began to hurt herself. She started by biting her hand and slamming her elbows on the edges of tables or doorframes and thus getting a shock. She used this strategy when she was anxious in order to calm herself. Her parents and school did however find it horrible to watch and hindered her physically. After a while she started to hit herself when she was anxious. The parents began to protect Jessica from hurting herself by making her wear metal arm stretchers. Then she started to slam her head in the wall. The protection was increased with soft walls and pillows and she spent most of her time fastened in her bed.
>
> When I entered the picture, Jessica was moving to a group home where the staff were not allowed to fasten her. Jessica was terrified when the safety devices were removed. She was afraid of her own arms. She had beaten herself bloody whenever she managed to get out of the body holders.

I have guided the work in several cases of this kind where a person early on has been hindered from minor self-injurious behaviour and consequently has developed a dangerous self-injurious behaviour. It is a difficult task to remove fastenings, but it is possible. We will discuss these methods later on in the book.

However, what I believe is the most important lesson from Jessica's and Christer's stories is that we must relate to whether the behaviour is dangerous and to why it is necessary. We can't remove a well-functioning strategy for difficult situations without replacing it with an equally good one. On the other hand, we may of course help the service-user finding a better strategy in the long run.

Cutting one's arm often has the same function as biting one's hand, but is more often seen in people with a higher level of function. The background, however, is the same, and the methods similar. In a project in Nottingham, they found that suicide rates increased if psychiatric patients were hindered from harming themselves, a discovery that has led to several ongoing studies of so-called 'safe self-harm', where the person is allowed to harm him- or herself and is offered sterile razor blades, first-aid kits and home nursing, to ascertain whether the quality of life of the service-user is improved.*

All these types of behaviour are not dangerous in themselves, even though they may be difficult for the people around the person in different ways. The task is therefore not to stop the specific behaviour, but to endure it and work with its causes. To step in immediately in the case of disobedience, abuse and non-dangerous behaviour is as meaningless as treating a headache when you have a brain tumour. It offers a temporary relief, but the causes are still there and the problems increase.

Later on in the book, in particular in the chapter on stress, I will discuss possible reasons for these types of behaviour, and how they can be dealt with through working with its causes.

Throwing the blame on somebody else

There is a mechanism that sometimes sets in motion when we find it hard to manage behaviours. We blame someone else! In some cases, we begin to talk about the service-user's problems and how he or she can't behave properly; in other cases, we begin to look for reasons for the behaviour in other people the service-user meets. Parents can blame friends and teachers, and teachers and preschool teachers have a tendency to blame the parents for the behaviour.

The problem with putting blame on somebody else is that that it means that you not only shirk responsibility, but also lose the possibility of exerting an influence. It is common to blame other

---

*   [No authors listed.] Australian Nurses Journal 2006.

people because you feel powerless, but by making other people responsible instead, you actually lose all power. Besides, it doesn't matter if you blame the child, the parents, the friends, the teacher or society. Only through taking on the responsibility for what you can influence, is it possible to exert an influence.

I am always a little suspicious when staff complain about parents; if they say 'Of course he can't manage school when he has to navigate that family' or 'With such a mother it can't really be expected that he develops normally'. I think that the staff simply don't know how to manage the pupil's behaviour. Consequently, I usually begin by asking everybody to write down their ideas of the family on a piece of paper. Then we keep the sheet until we have worked together for a while. If we still have the same ideas, we must report to social services and they can take care of it; if we on the other hand no longer find it difficult, we throw the piece of paper away. In the time in between we don't talk about the family.

This is often a good way to focus the staff's attention on what they can influence. I will illustrate this with the story of Paul.

Paul was 12 years old when I met him for the first time. He was born with a heart disease and was operated on when he was eight months old. In the operation he suffered a serious lack of oxygen and was brain damaged. As a 12-year-old he had a developmental age of 18 months. He used nappies and had great difficulties understanding the world around him. One of his greatest problems was that he was very sensitive to other people's feelings. If someone nearby was happy, he hit out. If someone was angry, he also hit out, as well as if someone was sad or loud.

Paul lived with his father who was an alcoholic. His mother had left when he was three years old and he had no contact with her. Paul attended special school with five other pupils until he was ten years old, when he got a classroom of his own with one teacher.

All through Paul's schooling they had talked about his father. Before Paul left for home every day he was given a clean nappy, and then he was changed when he was in school again. His nappies often were soiled, so the staff began to mark the nappies and discovered that his father did not change them, not even on weekends. The nappy Paul wore when he left school, he still had on when he was back at school, even after the weekend.

Paul went by taxi to and from school. His father was supposed to pick him up in the street as the family lived in a terraced house in a housing area where traffic was prohibited. Paul could not find his way home from the street. After half a year of schooling, a couple of neighbours reported that Paul often had to wait for hours for his father to pick him up. After that the taxi did not leave until Paul had been picked up. If he was not picked up within 15 minutes, they drove to the social services. Paul was at the social services at least once a week.

In school they often talked about the difficulties they experienced in the tutoring of Paul. The teachers were frustrated and resigned. They, however, spent a great deal of time on discussing the father and what could be done to make the social services pay attention to Paul's hard life. In three years, the staff of the school filed 20 reports to social services, without it having any effect.

When I entered the picture, we began by ending discussion of the father. We decided to file a last report in writing, and then we began to discuss how we could work with Paul. We started our work with the teachers relieving each other every second hour so they could stay completely calm all the time they were with him. Previously he had had the same teacher all day. After that we started working on these shifts of teachers so they were not hard for Paul. The next step was that the teachers gave him tasks and then sat outside his little room while he was working, so he could collect himself and concentrate on the task a few minutes at a time. Then we introduced a rewarding activity, to look at photos of his life. This led to his being able to concentrate for a longer period of time.

After a while the teachers started to like Paul, because the conflicts were reduced, and they connected with the mischievous boy he actually was.

After six months Paul had improved his attention, and he had on his own found a strategy to stay calm, despite other people's emotions; he had discovered that if he breathed slowly and deeply when other people were restless, he could stay calm. He could therefore return to the classroom with the other pupils.

The point is that Paul could not develop as long as the staff only talked about his father, but that his development was good when they dealt with what they could actually influence, which improved his quality of life considerably. Previously, the responsibility for Paul's development had been left to his father, who obviously could not take it on. I believe this mechanism arises when we don't find the tools and methods necessary; then we begin to look for other reasons, but forget that we at the same time shirk responsibility for the development and the educational or care work, and put it where we know nobody can take it on. We must take on responsibility if we are going to be able to exert an influence.

History: theories and therapies

Ever since challenging behaviour in people with different types of problems began to be described, reasons for the behaviour have been researched. In the 19th century several wild children, who were believed to have been living alone in the forest for years, were described, and their behaviour was considered to be more natural than the culturally adjusted behaviour of other people. The challenging behaviour was therefore considered more natural than ordinary behaviour, and through civilizing the children the behaviour would be changed. These accounts were largely due to romantic notions of nature in the 19th century, and today most scholars believe they were children with intellectual disabilities or autism that had been left in the woods shortly before being found.

Some time later a number of articles on heredity were published, which stated that criminal behaviour was hereditary. This was the background to the movement concerned with eugenics, where it was argued that the genetic quality of a people was dependent on those with intellectual disabilities or other problems not having children. In Sweden this led to a large number of sterilizations, and in the Germany of 1945 it resulted in there not being anyone with intellectual disabilities left; they had been exterminated.

The horror of these events naturally led to a discrediting of genetics as a useful explanation for behaviours that society finds difficult to accommodate. New explanations were needed.

Common ground for those models of explanation that won ground towards the end of the 1940s was that they all assumed that everyone (at least people of average intelligence) is born the same, and that behaviour and personality are affected by different factors after the birth. In Europe, psychoanalysis secured a strong foothold, and in the long run so did critical psychology. Psychoanalysis is founded on the idea that man's behaviour is a result of how we have solved a number of inner conflicts about sexuality, primarily in relation to our parents, whereas critical psychology sets out from behaviour being a result of how you have been affected by living in a capitalist society. In the US, behaviourism was the predominant truth with the idea that behaviour is the result of what you have learnt through conditioning.

When I attended university, psychoanalysis and behaviourism were considered exact opposites of each other. I think they are quite alike; they both assume that everyone is born alike and that we are affected by different factors at an early stage of life that form us as individuals. The development after the Second World War entailed dividing challenging behaviour into two groups:

- In people of average intelligence, challenging behaviour was considered the result of attachment disorders or poor or faulty upbringing. In any case it was the mother's fault.

- With intellectual disabilities, the mother could not be fully blamed, but certain attempts were made. Among other things the psychoanalyst Bruno Bettelheim described autism as the result of a 'fridge mother'. Most descriptions of behaviour from around 1970 consider challenging behaviour the result of the person lacking the necessary qualifications for behaving correctly.

This brought consequences to methods of treatment and to pedagogy. From the 1950s onwards play therapy and psychotherapy were used with those of average intelligence. Attempts to find methods to repair attachment disorders were also made. The most well-known of these is holding, where anxious children are held until they calm down to show the child that you are taking on responsibility for their anxiety. One of the most absurd examples is rebirth, where children were rolled up in rugs, then they waited for a couple of minutes, and pretended they were born again by pouring them out of the end of the roll, so they could start all over. If the children offered resistance, that was considered a good sign, as anger was believed to have a liberating effect. However, the use of such techniques has led to tragic results, as the case of Candace Newmaker shows.

> **Candace Newmaker** was adopted and had some challenging behaviours. Among other things she played with fire and killed goldfish. The parents sought assistance from two attachment therapists who recommended rebirth and holding therapy. When Candace was ten years old, in 2000, the parents and the therapists took part in rebirth treatment. She was rolled up in a rug, and the adults held her in place. She tried to get out, but failed, and she died of suffocation. The therapists Connell Watkins and Julie Ponder were afterwards sentenced to 16 years' imprisonment, and the parents were also sentenced to shorter terms of imprisonment.[*]

Luckily enough, these methods are no longer common. However, it is not unusual that a lack of upbringing is given as a reason for challenging behaviour. I have talked to many parents with children with autism or ADHD, whose grandparents have told their children that 'if you just let me take care of her for six months, you'll see she'll be just like anybody else'. They have received the same reception in school and in nursery, even if the children have had a diagnosis.

This kind of thinking has not been used with people with intellectual disabilities to the same extent. Instead methods based on ordinary upbringing have been used. People with an intellectual disability have been seen as children, and methods used on children have therefore been used. A great deal of scolding as well as punishment and consequential thinking have been prevalent.

---

[*]   Mercer, Sarner and Rosa 2006.

For a couple of years, I counselled staff in their work with adults with autism in an institution that previously had been part of a larger, old care institution. One of the employees told me that they had opened a new nursing home for elderly people with intellectual disabilities on the institution site. There was one problem though: the elderly women would not move into the nursing home; they refused to go through the doors.

Different solutions were attempted: their former staff accompanied them. The whole house smelled of delicious food. Entertaining music was played so it was heard outdoors. Nothing helped.

The reason for the women not wanting to enter the house was that in the 1970s it had been their isolation ward. There had been confinement cells fitted with rubber, and when the women disobeyed or were violent in their wards they were punished by solitary confinement for 24 hours to begin with. Moreover, emetics had been used, as it was believed that if the women associated sickness with their challenging behaviour, they would end the challenging behaviour.

In some cases the women were confined to the cells for up to a week, and were given emetics every day. Naturally there was a similar house for men.

Another member of staff told me that at her institution they had a lady in her sixties who always sat with one of her legs pulled up, so her calf lay to the back of her thigh. It looked uncomfortable, but she had been sitting like that for many years, and had difficulties sitting in another way. The reason was that in her youth she often tried to run away from her institution, and therefore for a number of years, after every attempted escape, her leg was tied up for a couple of months, so she could not leave.

Later on something happened with the attitude to challenging behaviour. Among other things it related to social progress in general.

I started school in 1972. I started in a traditional school. We had a teacher called Miss Jensen. She had no first name. We had a schedule that ruled the entire day. We had a schoolyard where you were supposed to be in the breaks, but no playground. The only entertainment in the schoolyard was a fountain with drinking-water in the middle of the ground. You quickly learnt to stick to the edges of the schoolyard so you did not end up in the fountain. In the schoolyard squares were painted for every class, and we started each day by singing a hymn, standing in the square of our class holding hands with a friend. Then the first graders would go inside, then the second graders, etc. If a fight arose the teacher on break duty would drag us to the first floor, where we had to talk to the headmaster. He would yell loudly and angrily, and that was the end of it.

My school was perhaps not the most modern, but it was well structured and clear. It didn't pay attention to the weakest pupils, but allowed some pupils to be there with their difficulties. If you had difficulties paying attention you were seated in the back of the classroom to watch out the window. Moreover, school offered a clear structure in daily life and did not require any self-management.

When I changed school and started fourth grade in 1975 everything changed dramatically. I had a new teacher. He was called Sven and wore overalls at work, wore a full beard and smoked a pipe. Sven did not consider schedules important, and he did not send pupils to the headmaster's. Sven thought we should discuss the conflicts instead of telling us off. He also liked teamwork. He often asked for our opinions.

This development was not limited to my schooling, but was a tendency in society in general. Since the early 1970s the demands on self-management have increased tremendously in school and in working life. When my eldest daughter started school in 1993 she started in a mixed-age class where there was no set schedule, but every pupil had to take responsibility for his or her own learning of Swedish and maths, and then present a project every month with at least one friend. When she had a conflict with another child she had to, in class, discuss what went wrong and other possible solutions. She had some difficulties concentrating, but was not allowed to sit in the back, but in the front.

This development has continued. Today school makes much greater demands on the ability to structure, take in situations and assess others' and your own behaviour. At the same time all pupils have to live up to centrally made demands.

As early as the late 1970s, discussions on certain pupils not having the abilities needed to pass school despite normal intelligence were raised. Concepts like MBD (minimal brain damage) were often mentioned in the debate and more pupils than ever before were placed in treatment facilities to repair what their parents had ruined.

In the early 1980s discussions on concepts like Asperger's syndrome and DAMP (Deficits in Attention Motor and Perception) began, and in the 1990s the diagnoses Asperger's syndrome and ADHD were acknowledged in the World Health Organization (WHO)'s International Classification of Diseases and in the American Psychiatric Association (APA)'s diagnostic manual.

What actually happened in the 1990s was that it was suddenly OK to have problems, despite being of average intelligence and not brain damaged. In the period from 1950 to the 1990s it was believed that if a person was of average intelligence and had challenging behaviour it probably was the mother's or society's fault (if European) and a fault in learning (if American). Now a possible reason was hereditary problems with communicative abilities or attention.

To understand this, it is vital to understand the workings of diagnoses. Most often doctors make a diagnosis, and they only do so if there is a problem. All psychiatric diagnoses have one main criterion: there must be a problem coping in your daily life.

We are lucky that is the case, otherwise all of us would probably have the diagnosis OCD (obsessive-compulsive disorder), as we all have compulsive behaviour at times. Who hasn't checked that the door is locked three times when leaving for work, and who hasn't gone looking for the iron to make sure the flex is unplugged before going on holiday, even though it has been a while since it was last used?

In my first lecture on psychopathology in university our teacher asked us to discuss how many times it was OK to check if the coffee maker had been turned off before it was unhealthy. Personally I don't have that kind of compulsive behaviour so I reckoned that if you had seen that it was turned off, it was unhealthy to check it again. The woman beside me thought it was probably too much if you checked more than ten times. The correct answer is of course that you can check as many times as you need, if you still are able to manage your life, but that if it stops you from going to work it is too much.

If you can't manage daily life because of compulsive behaviour, hallucinations, difficulties in concentration or problems with flexibility or social interaction, you risk being sent to a psychiatrist. His or her task is to analyse why you can't manage daily life. This is described in a diagnosis. The psychiatrist must make a diagnosis, for the simple reason that the main common criterion has been met. By referring somebody, someone has already defined that there is a problem in daily life. This aspect the psychiatrist doesn't have to look into. The psychiatrist is only supposed to find out why there is a problem with managing daily life. This means that the character of daily life has an influence on who is referred to diagnostic assessment.

Charles was born in the 1930s. He started school in the early 1940s and managed reasonably well. He was a slightly special boy who did not play much with the other children, but who liked to be at home at the farm. He was very interested in trains, cars and tractors and started at an early age to collect tools. After compulsory school he began to work at a machine station where he repaired machines and drove a combine harvester in autumn and snowplough in winter.

Charles's parents died when he was a young man, so he never left home. He just took over the farm. He never got married but was known as a good man you could always rely on and who was willing to help if you needed some advice on a car repair or the like. He was slightly peculiar and did not like new people for the first couple of years, but got used to them in time.

When Charles died and somebody entered his house they found something beyond comprehension. Charles had been collecting tools of the brand Bahco, and he had all hand tools that had been produced by Bahco in the 20th century. He did not have only one of each, but several hundreds of them. There were 224 Phillips 3mm screwdrivers, 263 4mm and 320 5mm. There were 260 ordinary hammers and 312 new, unused handsaws.

It is true Charles did well in life, and probably had not had more problems than most in life, but today we would still say that

he probably had Asperger's syndrome. However, he did not need
a diagnosis, as he did not experience problems in daily life.

Towards the end of the 1970s and all of the 1980s there were
discussions on certain pupils not managing at school. These pupils had
problems reminiscent of those of children with autism. Conceptions
like high-functioning autism were introduced for children with a
behaviour reminiscent of autism despite being of average intelligence
and having reasonably normal linguistic skills. The reason was
schools' development towards greater demands on self-management,
which affected children with certain problems around structure and
social intercourse. School and parents sent these children to child
psychiatry clinics, and psychiatrists started to discuss whether there
were more and more children with autism. The concept of Asperger's
syndrome was brushed up (it had previously been described in a
dissertation in German from 1944) and in 1992 WHO and APA
decided to approve the diagnoses Asperger's syndrome, pervasive
developmental disorder not otherwise specified (PDD-NOS) and
attention-deficit hyperactivity disorder (ADHD).

However, this development entailed that we had to change our
view of challenging behaviour. Some of those children that had been
believed to have challenging behaviour because of their mother's care
and her contact with the child when little suddenly had a diagnosis.
The staff at nursery or in school could no longer separate behaviour
according to intelligence; most people who are diagnosed with
autism today are of average intelligence. At first people discussed
that some children had autism or ADHD and attachment disorders.
It was believed that the need of special education was due to the
neuropsychiatric problems, and that the behaviour was attachment-
related.

That did not work in the long run. In some childcare services over
50 per cent of the children have a neuropsychiatric diagnosis. A child
may be entered before he or she has got a diagnosis and is dealt with
from a perspective of attachment disorder. Then the child is referred
to a child psychiatry clinic and diagnosed with, for example, ADHD.
This does not of course mean that the reason for the behaviour has

changed, but that the staff are given another explanation and have to change their ideas of the child and the behaviour.

A new outlook

Because of this development, neuropsychologist Ross W. Greene redefined the reason for challenging behaviour completely. Among other things he worked with guidance and counselling in juvenile prisons in the state of Maine in the US. At the time the relapse rate of criminality was 80 per cent and consequence-oriented methods were primarily used in a rough environment. Ross Greene began by starting out from a simple explanation of behaviour: people will do the right thing if they can. His work resulted in the percentage of relapse dropping to nearly half the amount. His view and outlook on people is:

People who can behave, will.

The key word is *can*. It is about ability, not free will. On the whole I believe that free will is overrated, but we will come back to that later on.

This way of thinking means that if someone has challenging behaviour, the demands are probably set too high. The person doesn't have the prerequisites to live up to the demands. These demands can come from members of staff, or him- or herself, or they can be demands that are embedded in culture, for example being quiet in the bus or managing to sit still in the classroom for at least 20 minutes at a time.[*]

The most common demands I see as reasons for challenging behaviour in my work are:

- demands on executive functions
- demands on communication skills
- demands on overall view
- demands on patience

---

[*]   Greene 1998.

- demands on flexibility
- demands on empathic ability
- demands on acquiescence
- demands on surplus.

Demands on executive functions and understanding of contexts

We expect people to understand the consequences of their actions. Some people don't and this often brings about great difficulties in their lives.

> **Henry** starts a new school, in a special unit. He is 14 years old and has had problems in his former school. He has always found it difficult not to end up in a conflict and has skipped school frequently in the last year.
>
> On his first day in school Henry has a conflict with a schoolmate, Oscar. They hit each other with their fists and Henry gets a black eye. Oscar gets a big bump in his forehead. When the teacher has calmed them down he asks Henry who started. 'It was Oscar,' says Henry, 'he hit me back when I head-butted him.'

Henry doesn't see immediate contexts in everyday situations. He doesn't understand Oscar's motive because he doesn't see it in context with his own behaviour. Over 90 per cent of cases that end up on my desk have a passage about the service-user not understanding the consequences of his or her behaviour. We will deal with this in detail later on.

Demands on communication skills

Many people with neuropsychiatric problems have difficulties with communication. In service-users with a great need for assistance this is seen as a lack of linguistic development, whereas in people with a higher level of function it is seen as difficulties understanding what is implied in the communication.

Manuel is 42 years old. He has autism and has throughout his youth been very violent. He lives in a group home with two women of the same age. Manuel's language skills are extremely limited; he can say coffee, sweets and cookie. Every time he tries to make contact with the staff one of these words is used.

New employees say no if it is not time for coffee/sweets/ cookies. Manuel doesn't like the word no and can get anxious, and sometimes violent when he gets a no. The experienced staff know that most of the time he is only trying to make small talk, and that this is hard when you only have three words to choose from. Their response to his coffee coffee coffee is therefore: yes, Manuel, coffee is good. Then Manuel is pleased.

Demands on overall view

In our assessments of youths with a criminal behaviour in custody and youth correctional facilities we have seen an apparent pattern in Rorschach-results. In general, everybody stands out in the factor called CDI (coping deficit index). This means that they have difficulties surveying situations they are part of and often deliberately limit their focus to make it easier to do so. Their actions are consequently often based on limited information, and may therefore seem incomprehensible to the uninitiated.

Tariq is 16 years old and has Asperger's syndrome. He is very sensitive to other people touching him, not least because his teachers restrained him more than 500 times in elementary school. Tariq commutes by train, but rarely buys a ticket.

The situation in question arises because Tariq sees a ticket inspector enter the train. Therefore, he leaves the train at once. The inspector follows him onto the platform and asks to see his ticket. Tariq doesn't think he has to show his ticket on the platform and says so. He turns around and leaves.

The inspector grabs hold of Tariq's shoulder, which makes Tariq turn around and bite the inspector's arm. Two more inspectors arrive and keep a firm hold of him until the police arrive and take over. In the course of events Tariq lies on the ground screaming: 'Don't rape me, don't rape me.'

Afterwards Tariq says that he doesn't understand why only he is being prosecuted and not the inspectors. The inspector started it; he was simply defending himself. He has no understanding that you can't bite inspectors: 'Them wearing a uniform only makes me more scared,' he says.

Demands on patience

Many conflicts arise from situations of waiting or in situations that require patience in other ways. People with developmental problems often find it hard to wait and easily become restless. Likewise they may have incredible difficulties carrying through something that requires deeper studies and concentrating on a task for more than a few minutes.

> **Tom** is a teacher in special school. He and a colleague are on an excursion in the forest with eight children. After a pleasant excursion they are being picked up by the school's minibus. However, the bus only has eight seats and they are ten people. It is decided that Tom will stay with two children who will be picked up by the bus later. Tom and the two children wave to the other children. Afterwards Tom gives the children one sweet each and says: 'Here you are for being so good at waiting.'

Tom helps the children endure the waiting by diverting them with a sweet, and praises them at the same time. He doesn't place the responsibility with the children, but takes it on himself.

Demands on flexibility

Some people in the neuropsychiatric field have great difficulties with continuous adjustment in daily life. They have difficulties changing track, and often want to try to hold on to one point of view when others try to make them change their mind.

> **Maya** is nine years old and has ADHD. She attends school close to her home, in a regular class. She does well in most circumstances, but sometimes things are too difficult for her. One day she is going on an excursion with her class. They are taking

the train to a museum in a city nearby. It is decided that the class will be back at the station at 3pm. Maya's mother will pick her up at the station to minimize Maya's stress; it is hard enough for her going away, and another change for picking-up at school would probably be too much. The other children will go back to school afterwards to finish off and then go home by themselves.

Unfortunately it rains all day. Everything goes well initially, the trip with the train is fine, but when the class walks from the station to the museum they are soaked through. All pupils are slightly dejected, and it is hard for the teachers to keep the children calm, so they go home earlier than decided. However, nobody has thought of contacting Maya's mother, and Maya herself doesn't know the time.

When the train arrives at the station at home Maya's mother is therefore nowhere to be seen. Maya is very concerned and starts to talk loudly about her mother not being there, and wants the class to stay and wait with her. The teacher tells her that is not possible, which makes Maya start screaming and telling the teachers off for not keeping the time as decided. One teacher defends himself by saying that she must keep a check on things herself, and that she actually does know the way home. Maya kicks him on the shin, screams and cries, and runs away.

Maya is not able to adjust to the change of plan. She gets into a state of anxiety and reacts. When her teacher then begins to discuss the matter with her, her unease increases and she reacts with challenging behaviour. She lacks the necessary resources for meeting the demands of those around her.

Demands on empathic ability

It is not only people with autism who find it hard to predict other people's intentions, but also people with other neuropsychiatric problems, as well as people with intellectual disabilities. If you can't predict what other people are thinking or imagine yourself in somebody else's shoes, you will show behaviour that other people find challenging.

> **Oscar** is 14 years old. He attends a special unit in elementary school, and is fairly happy with the situation. After school he usually goes to the newsstand to read porno magazines; he enjoys looking at naked girls.
>
> One day when he is standing reading a pornographic magazine an old lady hits him on the head with an umbrella. Oscar is very surprised and hits her back, but with his fist. The lady falls and is badly hurt, and the newsstand owner calls the police who arrive and bring Oscar in. Oscar thinks this is unfair as it was the lady who started it.
>
> Next day Oscar and his teacher discuss what happened. The teacher asks: 'Why did she hit you?' 'No idea,' says Oscar, 'I was just standing there reading. I hadn't done anything to her.' The teacher has a theory and asks: 'Could it be because you were reading a pornographic magazine?'
>
> Oscar thinks this over and realizes; 'Yeah, of course, she was probably thinking: "What do those girls have that I don't?"'

It is not hard to understand that Oscar has difficulties managing daily life. He is in need of clear assistance in social situations and finds it incredibly hard to predict other people's behaviour in everyday situations. He often has conflicts with people of his age.

> Another day Oscar is going to the park by bike. He passes six boys, a few years his senior, who are sitting drinking beer. Oscar has noticed them several times and thinks it would be fun to be with them as they are cool and exciting. When he cycles past them he therefore says: 'Hi girls.' They chase him up and give him a beating. Afterwards he asks: 'What did they do that for? They always call each other girls.'

Oscar's problem is that he finds it immensely hard to understand other people's motives, objectives and intentions. He acts from the patterns he understands and can relate to and has always had difficulties relating to there being differences between children and adults. His behaviour is a response to his conception of the world and his social perception and is not a problem in itself.

Difficulties with empathic skills can also cause challenging behaviour in other ways. Sometimes it is a matter of the service-user relating in a very concrete way to a rule and the like and not understanding other people's motives and intentions:

> **Isaac** has severe ADHD and attends a regular elementary school. One day all students in the intermediate level are going on an excursion and are collected in big tourist buses. The schoolyard is full of children; it is noisy and rowdy. A couple of teachers show the pupils which buses they should go to. Isaac is affected by the restlessness around him and feels that he wants to beat some of the unruly pupils close to him. Isaac's mother has taught him to go to an adult instead of hitting. Isaac sees his best friend's mother, Annie, who is standing in the crowd of parents waiting to wave goodbye to the children. Isaac stands right behind Annie and is immediately calmed; he relaxes and is indifferent again. No parents notice him standing there.
>
> Meanwhile panic breaks out among the teachers because Isaac suddenly has disappeared. It is a while before the parents, who are now talking among themselves, discover that Isaac is standing looking vacant behind Annie. Neither the teachers, the other pupils nor the parents understand why Isaac so suddenly up and left, and why he didn't react to the teachers calling for him. Isaac's teacher tells him off for not doing as he has been told. Isaac feels he has been truly wronged and is furious. He feels he has done exactly what he has been told.

Demands on acquiescence

The tendency to say yes or no is one of the character traits at which most interest has been directed at the last few years. One reason is that whereas projective personality tests have been used previously to describe and analyse people's personality characteristics, today questionnaires are being used. This means that a lot of questions are being asked. In the Minnesota Multiphasic Personality Inventory (MMPI)-2, which is the biggest clinical personality test, there are over 500 questions, and in NEO-PI-R, which is used both clinically and in employment contexts, there are 240 questions. When these tests were developed it was discovered that most people had a majority of *yes* replies; the answer yes was more frequent than no. This factor had to be taken into consideration in the development of the test, and so many of the questions are repeated, but inversely. The reply that was yes in the first question is no in the second. Then it is possible to measure the tendency to saying yes, which is called acquiescence, and evaluate the certainty of the other results.

Acquiescence is an important social skill. If everybody plays on the same team it is easier to get things done, and the survival rate has probably improved in an evolutionary context. Today we know that acquiescence is normally distributed and has a genetic component in the normal group, but also that many people with intellectual disabilities or neuropsychiatric disabilities have a pronounced reduced acquiescence. This means that they find it harder than other people to agree or say yes.

In daily life we take a high degree of acquiescence for granted. For example, we often say 'Would you like to eat now?' instead of 'Now it's time to eat'. The question is rhetorical; we don't expect a discussion and no actual answer, only that the person comes to eat. If the person has reduced acquiescence he may say no, because that is what he is able to in the situation, and we are annoyed. A low degree of acquiescence is often misunderstood as disobedience.

Endra was already as a small child palpably non-acquiescent. When her parents woke her up in the morning, they brought out clothes for her. She used to say no at once and take out clothes she picked herself. They were not always suited for the climate and weather. She could pick out miniskirts in the middle of the winter and refuse to put on her overalls as she was wearing a skirt. The parents solved the problem by bringing her two sets of clothes and saying: 'Good morning, Endra. Which of these sets of clothes would you like to wear today?'

Demands on surplus

The American scholars Isen and Levin's scientific work showed different factors that affect man's tendency to do the right thing. In 1972 they published a study where they had researched what happened with so-called surplus behaviour if met by a small misfortune in life. The setting was simple: absolutely unprepared inhabitants of an American city entered a phone booth to make a call. When the call was ended half of them were given extra change and half of them were given the right change. When they left the phone booth a young girl walked by and dropped a pile of paper in the street. The results showed that those who had received extra change helped her pick up the papers whereas most of the people who had not received any extra change walked straight past her without offering any help. Their surplus was not great enough to perform a surplus action.

If completely ordinary people are affected that much by such a small stroke of luck, how much then are people with developmental difficulties affected by misfortunes? How can we expect surplus actions, and can we expect kindness or other surplus behaviour at all?*

Thinking that it is the expectations and demands of the people close to the service-users in relation to the service-users' abilities that trigger challenging behaviour shifts the responsibility from the service-user to the staff or the parents. This is not a bad thing. Then we are given the possibility to influence. You can't influence anything if you don't take on responsibility.

We must learn to make reasonable demands. We must learn what problems and difficulties our service-users have, and we must deal with some of the notions we have of ourselves, the service-users and our methods.

Background to our conceptions

As human beings we have many different notions of ourselves, of other people and of behaviour. Unfortunately these don't always correspond with reality, but still have great consequences for the way we treat people in our daily life.

Many of our notions of people with intellectual or neuropsychiatric disorders are particularly faulty. That is due to us having learnt too little about people with difficulties.

---

*   Isen and Levin 1972.

Some who meet those with different difficulties are educated in working with people. They can be care staff, occupational therapists, teachers, social workers or psychologists. Unfortunately, what these educations have in common is that you don't learn what is necessary for working with people with intellectual disabilities or neuropsychiatric disorders. At least not regarding challenging behaviour.

They have often learnt something about ordinary children's development, perhaps Piaget's theories on cognitive development, perhaps Freud's theories on psychosexual development. Some people have learnt something about educational theories; perhaps concepts like Vygotsky's zone of proximal development or even Antonovsky's salutogenesis. However, they have rarely learnt much about different deviations from the ordinary, and at least not what to do if someone spits at them in the face. I studied at university for five years to be a psychologist. I learnt a lot about myself, the brain and ordinary development, and had three lectures on what one of our teachers called the 'limp and crippled'. Those were one lecture on deaf people, one on blind people and one on autism.

Similarly, as a parent to a child with special needs, you haven't learnt particularly much. You may have attended lectures on what is autism or met adults with autism who have talked about their lives. When someone speaks about autism they often only talk of the so-called triad of difficulties and diagnostics. You have very rarely learnt anything that is relevant in relation to managing your own child's behavioural disorders.

On the other hand, we have all learnt something about dealing with behavioural problems the few times we have displayed them ourselves. Perhaps we were two years old and refused to go to bed or we were 14 and had nicked chewing gum at Tesco's.

There is consequently a risk that what we know about managing challenging behaviour is something we have learnt during our own childhood. There is even a risk that we practise that type of behaviour management on our own children in our spare time if we are staff, or on our other children if we are parents to a child with difficulties. That kind of behaviour management we can call ordinary fosterage, and it usually works fine with ordinary children. The only problem with methods based on ordinary fosterage is that they don't work particularly well with people with intellectual disabilities, and not at all with people with neuropsychiatric disorders.

I would even assert that most people who have got a neuropsychiatric diagnosis have got it because ordinary methods of upbringing and disciplining haven't worked. Neither parents, nursery staff nor school teachers have managed to make these people do as expected with the methods normally used.

When a child grows up we use different methods for fosterage and teaching. As long as these work, everything in the garden is lovely. The second the methods don't work, we think the child has a problem. If they function so poorly that we have problems managing or teaching the children every day, we go to see a doctor or school psychologist. Then there is a risk (or chance) that the child is referred to further inquiry at a child psychiatry clinic. The psychiatrist's task is to describe why our methods don't work. That is done in a diagnosis. A good diagnosis offers guidance of what methods should be used instead of the ordinary methods, which have already proved not to work.

In most cases the staff at the child psychiatry clinic offer good guidance for teaching and sometimes also for limited behavioural disorders. However, guidance for how to understand and deal with severe behavioural disorders is rarely given.

This means that the reason for the children having been referred, that our ordinary methods of upbringing and disciplining don't work, is still in place. And we haven't been given alternative methods from the child psychiatry clinic. Consequently, there is a great risk that we feel unsure of what to do at this stage. Previously we had ordinary methods of upbringing. They didn't work. Now we know why, but we haven't been given other methods instead. The risk is that we continue using the non-working methods, and use the same strategy as some people do in contact with foreigners: if he doesn't understand what I say, I'll probably have to say it louder. If he still doesn't understand, it probably helps if I shout instead. Therefore we use these non-working methods more forcefully. More consequential thinking, more scolding, more punishment. As this still will not work, the frustration and the behavioural disorder will increase, and the relationship between child and parents/staff will deteriorate. In time the trust may become so low the child no longer trusts his or her parents or teachers at all. Then there is a risk that the child or youth trusts his or her friends more than adults, and then there is a risk of development of criminal behaviour or other more serious behavioural problems.

Working with, and in daily life with, children and youths with intellectual disabilities or neuropsychiatric difficulties, we must remember that most educational methods are developed for ordinary children. This means that we can't use them on children with intellectual disabilities or neuropsychiatric disorders straight off.

In the same way, theories and conceptions derived from ordinary methods of upbringing fall short.

Some of the things we learnt in our formal educations are not true for children and adults with intellectual disabilities or neuropsychiatric disorders either. Developmental theories are based on ordinary children most of the time. For example, Piaget only used observations of his own children when developing his theory on cognitive development. Some of his thoughts are therefore completely irrelevant to children with disabilities. For example, he said that people actively seek to create meaning. He meant that people always look for causal connections in their surroundings and thus create meaning and contexts in life. Unfortunately, this is only true for people within the spectrum of normality whereas people with autism, ADHD or intellectual disability don't in the same way. All educational methods that are based on the component of creating meaning are therefore not applicable in the field of special needs.

Some of the conceptions we have of our methods and of service-users originate from a psychoanalytical perspective as the dominant psychological paradigm in the decades after the Second World War. Other concepts often used concerning challenging behaviour are attachment and emotional damage. In this tradition, as discussed above, it was believed that everybody is born the same and that different social contacts influence development. Challenging behaviour therefore was considered the result of deficient social contacts, mostly described as the result of poor caring in infancy. The blame was mainly laid on the mother.

This way of thinking has been challenged from all directions in the last 20 years. Today we think there are genetic factors that can explain at least half of one's abilities and characteristics. The environment does of course play an important part, but not only the mother and the very beginning of life. On the other hand, it seems that friends from the teenage years have a substantial influence on certain traits of character, and that the development of personality continues all through life.*

However, some conceptions from psychoanalytical thinking still remain. The concept *catharsis* has become part of our common cultural heritage, despite the fact that the psychoanalysts stopped using it a long time ago. Catharsis means that it was believed that man's instincts could pile up and demand release in an emotional outburst. After the Second World War several therapeutic methods based on catharsis were developed, including holding therapy, gestalt therapy and primal scream therapy. Some of the basic 'truths' of these forms of therapy have become established truths in our culture. Among other things most people believe that it is important to give vent to one's feelings, and people are encouraged to beat pillows if they are frustrated. Unfortunately, there is no scientific evidence of this working.

Likewise we have pedagogical 'truths' like 'you must own your conflict', 'only take the conflict you can win' and that 'you must be consistent with children with challenging behaviour'. These conceptions are derived from attachment theory, where one of the principles is to be able to trust staff and adults in general, and one of the methods is that staff and adults take responsibility for the child or service-user by protecting him or her from uncertainty. Adults and staff are strong and always win, and if an adult or staff says something, then that is true. We will deal with this way of thinking later on and relate it to reality and what we know of neuropsychiatry and intellectual disability.

Furthermore, some of the conceptions from the old European outlook on people that led to hundreds of thousands of sterilizations,

---

*   In the book *The Blank Slate: The Modern Denial of Human Nature* (2002), Steven Pinker has summarised research and theory formation about this in a readable and easily accessible way.

and in Germany to the extermination of people with intellectual disabilities in the 1930s and 1940s, are still in place, and even now affect our way of handling the human rights of people with disorders.

> **Karen** is 30 years old and lives in Denmark. She has severe physical functional disorder and is in a wheelchair. She is spastic and is therefore not able to speak, but communicates through BLISS (a visual symbilc communication system). On her 18th birthday she looked forward to voting for the first time. At the first election after her 18th birthday she was sent her electoral card and went to the polling station with her mother on election day. The presider at the poll asked her how she was going to vote. Her mother told him that they would enter the polling booth together and that she would help Karen. The presider said: 'That's unfortunately not possible. She has to do it on her own; you may not join her.' The mother asked if one of the presiders could help her, but they were not allowed either. Karen had to go home without voting.
>
> Karen and her mother made a complaint to the local authorities and got the reply: 'Every voter must be able to vote on her or his own. Karen is entitled to vote and will therefore be sent an electoral card, but she will probably be turned away at the polling station.' Since then Karen has voted by post with her mother. Nobody discovers anything that way.

When we work with people with intellectual disabilities or neuropsychiatric disorders we must be very observant not to remove our service-users' rights. There is a long history of abuse, and it is easy to continue on the same track. For example, many people in care feel it is OK to use violence and restraints or control holds on service-users in difficult situations, like when a service-user wants to run away. We would never have the same attitude to restraints on ordinary people if they wanted to run away. Most of us have even taught our children to run away rather than fight.

In the same way parents must remember that their children will grow up even though they will not make it on their own as adults. As parents, we can't remove the rights of our adult children, for example fertility, only because we feel responsible. We must use the systems society has set and allow other people to take over where we can't let go of the control ourselves. Otherwise there is a great risk that we keep 'parenting' the children and limit dangers by taking over where other people would not have been as overprotective. Because of that, I believe it is unfortunate if relatives are trustees or personal assistants to grown people with functional disorders.

If we are to change our automatic and faulty conceptions and our methods of working we have to identify them and find out their origin.

Summary

Challenging behaviour can be defined in different ways. In this book I use the definition 'behaviour that causes problems for people around the person'. The people around the person with disabilities experience problems when they do not have the methods necessary to deal with the behaviour. We must therefore learn and develop the methods needed in order to take responsibility, if we are to work in the field of special needs.

This way of thinking is supported by the idea that 'People who can behave, will'. Often challenging behaviour is the result of the staff or parents having made too high demands on the service-user. In order to minimize challenging behaviour we must minimize our demands on abilities like executive functioning, acquiescence, communication skills and flexibility.

In order to do so we may have to change some of our conceptions that stem from our own upbringing and education, where focus is often on the psychology of average people. People with intellectual disabilities or neuropsychiatric disorders are not average, which means that we should ignore broad theories of development and methods of normal fosterage.

Chapter 2
• • • • • • •
Conceptions and Misconceptions

The importance of self-control

There are various different conceptions and misconceptions that influence our and our service-users' behaviour. Perhaps the most important common misconception is that as parents or staff you have or can take control over the service-users. If you feel you lose control over a service-user, you would normally try to gain it again as soon as possible. Then there is a risk of using force, for example by grabbing the service-user or forcing a contact.

As a matter of fact, nobody can have the control over another human being. The other person must be in full control of him- or herself in order to entrust even a part of him- or herself to somebody else. The service-user must therefore be in full control of him- or herself if you as a member of staff or a parent are to feel secure and in control.

To illustrate this we will look at two situations experienced by Angel.

Angel is 12 years old. She has Down's syndrome with slight intellectual impairment and attends special school. Angel sometimes finds it hard to take in the social situations she is a part of. She can become anxious if something she has not foreseen happens. She also gets anxious if her teachers or parents make demands she is not prepared for.

One Tuesday afternoon Angel plays with some classmates. They are loud and a teacher tells them to stop. Angel does not respond, but continues being noisy and laughing. The teacher approaches Angel, grabs her arm and says: 'You must stop now, Angel, you're being too loud.'

Angel walks backwards, looking frightened. The teacher follows, which causes Angel to hit out at the teacher: 'Go away, go away, leave me be,' Angel says and looks away.

'Look at me when I'm talking to you,' the teacher says and grabs Angel again. Angel kicks her, hits out right and left and starts crying. The teacher pulls Angel to the couch and makes her sit down, whereupon Angel once again hits and kicks. Two teachers have to hold Angel until she calms down, which takes eight minutes. Afterwards the teacher reads Angel a story.

Another Tuesday afternoon Angel is playing with some classmates. They are once again loud and a teacher tells them to stop. Angel does not respond, but continues being noisy and laughing. Then the teacher approaches Angel and tells her: 'You must stop now, Angel, you're being too loud.'

Angel walks backwards, away from the teacher, looking frightened. The teacher takes two steps backwards and has a seat on the couch. She looks away from Angel and finds a storybook. Angel stays in place for a short while, until she has regained control, whereupon she sits down next to her teacher on the couch. Then they read a story.

What happened to Angel was that she lost self-control for a short while. Her first strategy to regain control was to move away from the teacher: it can be difficult to stay in control if somebody else is too close, especially in stressful situations. The teacher's interference came abruptly to Angel, and consequently she tried to survey the situation and become calm as fast as possible. Often this is done by limiting sensory impressions, for example by looking away, creating a distance or shutting oneself out.

The difference between these two situations is that the first time the teacher thinks she has to gain control over Angel to ensure her calming down. She therefore follows Angel, grabs her and tries to force eye contact. In reality she ruins Angel's chances of regaining control of herself, and by that the possibility for Angel to entrust some of this control to the teacher. The consequence is a stressful situation for Angel, the teachers and the other pupils, and an unnecessary and illegal use of force.

The second time, the teacher leaves Angel room to regain self-control, both by walking backwards and by sitting down looking away, and at the same time offers her a way out through the storybook.

Common strategies to regain control of oneself include:

- refusing or saying no in a demanding situation if you have difficulties foreseeing the consequence of saying yes

- taking a few steps away from the other people; when under stress our need for personal space increases

- creating a distance to the other people by hitting out, throwing things or screaming to keep them away

- shutting off mentally in order to be less affected by those around you

- running away

- biting your hand or arm so you can focus on the pain and ignore other impressions

- cutting your arm

- using threats or taunts to be acknowledged.

All these behaviours are positive, forward-looking strategies to regain or keep self-control. In many contexts they are however considered challenging behaviour because the staff feel they lose control for a short while. If staff react forcefully or confrontingly in these situations, dangerous, violent situations that the service-users often are blamed for may arise.

One factor that comes into play regarding self-control is the level of affect. No matter what the feelings are, whether positive like happiness or negative like anger, it is best if they are in moderation. The small child is a highly affective being that harbours grand feelings. You are tremendously happy when happy and awfully sad when sad. The grand feelings however entail that the child loses self-control and screams and cries or is so happy that he or she must bite. It is easy to see in preschool-age children that have to be kept calm: if an adult plays rowdily with them they are overwhelmed and it often ends in tears. Figure 2.1 can be used to understand self-control in relation to affect.

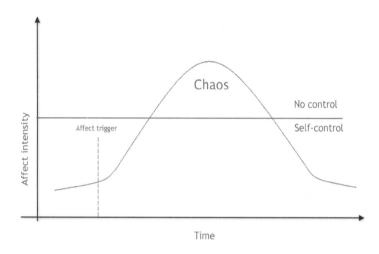

Figure 2.1 Self-control and the intensity of affect

At the beginning of the course of events the level of affect is low and the service-user has full self-control. Then something happens. It can be an external event, for example that somebody takes one's cap. What once happened to one of my clients was that she was offered two flats at the same time. One flat would have been a good event, but two meant that she could no longer act. Her level of affect rose rapidly and she was about to lose self-control, but kept it through scratching her arm bloody.

If the level of affect rises too rapidly, the control is lost, and we have what is sometimes called an outburst of affect. After a while it passes and the service-user regains self-control. The older we get, the better we are at adjusting our affect. Some psychologists believe that maturity can be defined as the ability to regularize affect. Among others, the psychologist Daniel Stern has written a good deal about the development of personality and regularization of affect. If we accept that our service-users have not reached a maturity corresponding to their age, we must expect their ability of affect regulation to be reduced and accordingly adjust our pedagogy.

In our work we must focus on the service-users' self-control. Our methods must aim for the service-users to stay in control of themselves as much as possible. Our service-users do wish to cooperate, but in order to do so they must have enough self-control to be able to trust us with some control as well. Daily life must be characterized by cooperation and not by staff's control over the service-users.

We will return to this way of thinking in more detail below, in a more developed model of mental load and stress. We will also look at a method for solving conflicts focusing on how staff can use affective methods to strengthen the service-user's self-control.

There are, however, certain factors that can help us keep our self-control. Trust is one of these. It is much easier to stay calm when you are with someone you trust.

The following situation is an example of this:

> **You** are on your way to the delivery ward to give birth. You have your husband with you. When you arrive, you are met by a midwife in the door who says: 'Hi there! You're coming with me and your husband will sit over there in the father room. There you'll find magazines with trucks, motorbikes and other things men like. There are even a few magazines with pictures of naked ladies. In the delivery room we have a male counsellor who is really good at holding hands so the father won't be needed.'

Of course it would not feel as good holding hands with a strange man during a delivery. We do not bring the partner for him to experience the delivery, but mostly because you need someone you trust when going through something that is really hard. Rather a happy amateur who faints in the middle of everything and hides behind the camera than a professional hand-holder. A delivery is one of the most difficult experiences a woman goes through in life, and it is important she has somebody with her she trusts so she can endure it.

Working in the field of special needs we must relate to trust as an important factor for pedagogy and care. We must be able to evaluate our methods from a point of view of trust: do my methods bring a greater trust or do they reduce it? When doing so I believe that we have to be very concrete. We must relate to whether the service-users are angry with us or consider us unfair, as this might reduce the trust. If the service-users think we are being unfair, we probably are in an pedagogical sense.

Previously, I wrote that we must act according to whether our methods create self-control, and we must likewise act according to whether our methods create trust. If the service-user reacts violently to our interventions, they probably do not create trust. Poor interventions upset the trust instead, just as they ruin the service-users' self-control and our opportunities of influencing the service-user in a positive way.

Methods for changing behaviour

We have different conceptions of our methods and some of them are not conscious. Often it is a matter of us not having consciously learnt to manage challenging behaviour, leaving us to act only with our gut feelings or according to what we experienced in our own childhood. We will look at a few different methods of behaviour management.

Scolding

Scientific studies have shown that mothers tell their toddlers off a little bit more than once a minute when in the supermarket. At home it is slightly less, but still six or seven times an hour or more. This happens in spite of the fact that scientific studies never have proven that scolding has a positive effect. Often you feel you can interrupt a behaviour by telling the child off, but that does not mean the behaviour will not be repeated. Rather, scolding might actually have a mainly diverting effect; it is hard to continue your behaviour when someone is telling you off.

Unfortunately, scolding has been shown to have some negative effects:

- *Lack of enthusiasm.* People who have been told off a lot have difficulties becoming absorbed in something. Regrettably, this rarely means they are scolded less in the long run. There is a considerable risk that we start a negative circle. Part of the enthusiasm may concern self-esteem, but may also be a result of decreasing trust to the scolder. Pupils therefore do worse in school if they are told off.

- *Poor ability to concentrate.* Poor power of concentration is not always due to that, but it is worth considering that some of the people we scold the most are children with a lack of ability to concentrate. If you tell a child with ADHD off you weaken their poorest abilities.

- *Poor endurance.* Once again, do we want our service-users to have a harder time waiting for example?

- *Depression and low self-esteem.* It is easy to draw this conclusion if we remember what it was like being told off as a child. When you are scolded or reprimanded you are often overwhelmed by the shame, and repeated feelings of shame weaken your self-esteem. You are acknowledged by not being good enough, which in time can be devastating.

- *Somatic problems.* Those who are told off more frequently than other people unfortunately develop illnesses that require medical treatment more often. This must mean that scolding is harmful and is difficult to make excuses for. Some of the points above can themselves be the reasons for being told off, but it is difficult to use that argument on physical illnesses. We probably scold sick people less than others.[*]

If, instead of telling off, you describe what to do in a similar situation another time, the result is often better. It works best if you help the service-user realize what could have worked better. However, it is important to let go of anger. You cannot give behavioural directions when cross because most people will not understand what you are saying if you are angry. The Danish psychologist Erik Sigsgaard carried out studies of scolding in the 1990s. One of his findings was that in 50 per cent of the cases the ordinary children did not know why they had been told off. They were not capable of listening because of the adults' anger. It is no doubt at least just as difficult

---

[*]   Sigsgaard 2003, 2007.

for children or adults with neuropsychiatric problems or intellectual disabilities.

Reprimands

Recent research has shown that reprimands work differently in adults and children of average intelligence. In an interesting study participants of different ages were given a test where you were supposed to learn from your experiences. They were going to sort cards on a computer screen and every time they did it correctly the computer said 'right' and every time the cards were sorted wrongly it said 'wrong'. The aim of the test was to see how people learnt from feedback. In this study the blood flow in the brain was also monitored to see whether the subjects learnt most from being told that they had done right or wrong.

The results proved to be different in different ages. When children up to 15 years old got negative feedback (you did wrong), they did not react by thinking. The brain did not show any increased activity and it did not particularly affect their results in the tests. When they were given positive feedback (you did right) the brain activity increased and the results immediately improved. In adults the pattern was reversed.

This means that children learn by being told that they have done correctly, whereas adults learn from their mistakes. This is not as strange as it might seem at first. Man learns from discrepancies from expectation. We do not remember what we did on 27 September 2001, but we know exactly what we did on the 11th. That day was different from other days because the World Trade Center in New York was subjected to a terror attack. That was a discrepancy from daily life, and we remember the day. To children, doing wrong is no discrepancy. They do wrong all the time. Therefore they do not respond to negative feedback. They shrug their shoulders and move on. If children were to care about doing wrong, they would never learn what children actually learn. You must work on something you are very bad at for many hours every day for months or years without any particular result until suddenly there is an effect; for example, learning to speak, playing a musical instrument or reading.

Adults on the other hand are used to doing right. We piece our daily life together and are good at what we do at work. When we fail it is a discrepancy from what we are used to. Consequently adults learn from their mistakes.[*]

Our service-users are not used to doing right. They are used to errors and mistakes. Therefore we cannot expect them to learn from their mistakes. They simply learn better when we tell them what they did correctly. We should quit using reprimands as a method. They, unfortunately, only confirm that you are pretty useless at what you are doing. Instead we should tell them when they do something right. We should praise them and give positive feedback. Instead of red marks in the maths book, there should be a big R at every correctly solved task.

Punishment

We often use punishments, even though we sometimes call it something else. Educational and care staff frequently talk about consequences instead.

> **Joseph** is 19 years old and has autism. He is interested in liquids and, among other things, likes to play with water and washing-up liquid on the draining board. One day he pees on the floor in the bathroom. The staff talk the situation through and decide that he must mop up after himself so he learns not to pee on the floor. Joseph likes mopping and starts to pee on the floor every day and now no longer only in the bathroom.

> **Eric** is 12 years old and has ADHD. He nicks sweets in a shop close to home. The staff discover him and call the police who drive him home. Eric's mother is furious. She decides to ground him for two weeks and does not let him play video- or computer games in this time. Her argument is that this will deter him from shoplifting in the future. Eric thinks she is being very unfair and sulks, quarrels and is a nuisance in general the whole period.

---

[*] van Duijvenvoorde *et al.* 2008.

> **Sybil** is 56 years old and has an intellectual disability. Sometimes she has days when she is difficult and calls out a lot. Such days the staff threaten to take away her coffee if she does not calm down and often her coffee is removed.

Punishment has been part of society for centuries. All civilizations have used punishment, from the stoning in the Law of Moses, the Roman slave ships and the fines of the Viking Age to the fines and imprisonments of today. Ancient laws often used the principle of an eye for an eye and a tooth for a tooth, as the punishment was to correspond to the deed.

For centuries it has been known that punishment does not have the desired effect on the person punished. That has not been necessarily the reason for the punishment either. In the ancient laws of Scandinavian countries the reason was that the person subjected to the crime should be compensated, so fines paid out to the victim was the most common punishment. The severe punishments of the Old Testament can be seen as a way of solving the problem permanently; a person condemned to death will not relapse into crime. Another argument has been that we must punish those who deserve it. Otherwise God will punish us collectively.

Sometimes punishment may even legitimize and increase challenging behaviour. In a quite recently published article, the story of an Israeli day care centre is told. Sometimes children were picked up too late from the day care centre, which put the staff in a difficult spot. They could not go home until the children were picked up. In order to prevent this situation, they introduced a fine for picking up a child too late. Surprisingly enough, that doubled the incidents of parents being late. The reason for this might be that the fine, a punishment, provided a legitimate structure for being late. It is OK to be late if you pay the price.[*]

In the field of special needs we see this pattern all the time. From early childhood the service-users have been punished over and over again, and have adapted to that structure. They expect a punishment, but the punishment does not have any lasting effect on their behaviour. In the light of the Israeli day care story, it is clear

---

[*]   Gneezy and Rustichini 2000.

that there is no reason to punish if the same punishment has been used over and over again and the behaviour still pops up from time to time.

Some of us bring this principle into our own lives. It is quite common to speed, driving perhaps ten miles an hour too fast. If we get caught we pay the price, but few of us feel bad about the behaviour, we just do not like being caught. We might even park illegally from time to time, but we direct our bad feelings not towards the act but towards the traffic wardens.

Punishment does however have one positive effect: a general preventative effect. This means that if society punishes someone it sometimes will affect everybody around him or her so the risk of others doing what the person is being punished for decreases. For example, suppose you are driving at 75 miles an hour where the speed limit is 70. After a while you drive by an unmarked police car with the blue lights on that has stopped a young man driving a BMW. What happens then? You release the pressure on the accelerator and drive at 70 miles an hour for about five minutes. Then you speed again. Why do you do that? The police rarely have two unmarked cars out at the same time. The most logical action would be to increase the distance from the police as fast as possible so they will not catch up with you later on. But instead you slow down. The reason for your behaviour is that you know that what is true for young men in BMWs is true for you as well. You have the same behaviour and see somebody being punished. That affects your behaviour.

In order for there to be a general preventative effect you must have the ability to understand that what is true for other people is true for you as well. Furthermore, the behaviour punished must be one you could engage in as well. Therefore the general preventative effect works on speeding but not murder. If the punishment for murdering your partner was decreased to six months of imprisonment it would not have any effect at all on my life. I would never kill my partner anyway.

The problem with using punishment in relation to people with intellectual disabilities or neuropsychiatric disorders is that

- it does not work on the person punished

- it might even create a structure around the behaviour and thereby increase it

- it unfortunately does not work on the person sitting next to the person if he has an intellectual disability or neuropsychiatric disorder.

The reason for this last part is that people with intellectual disabilities or neuropsychiatric disorders are not part of the concept of *general*. They are not 'ordinary'. Many of them have difficulties understanding that what is true for the person sitting next to them, probably is true for them as well. Therefore there is no preventative effect of punishment at all in the group.

To punish someone with developmental disabilities in order to get a general preventative effect, for example in a mainstream school, is usually not logical either.

> **Hugo** has ADHD. He goes to a regular elementary school. One day he breaks a window in the canteen. He is summoned to the headmaster who tells him he must pay for a new pane of glass. The reason for this is that the headmaster partly wants to influence him not to break windows again, partly wants to lessen other pupils' tendency to break windows.

We know that Hugo will not break fewer windows in the future if he is punished. We also know that most other children will not break windows at school at all. Besides, we also know that the other children who sometimes break windows are not fully aware that what is true for Hugo is also true for them. The effort is consequently pointless.

Unfortunately, several studies have even proved that punishment often leads to criminality in the long run.[*] It is distressing that it is like that, and it must influence our decisions. Punishment therefore has no place in special schools, residential placements, daily life therapy, special units within mainstream schools, treatment facilities or other facilities established to care for people with special needs.

---

[*]   Frank 1983; Gershoff 2002; Solomon and Serres 1999.

Consequential thinking

A commonly used concept in managing challenging behaviour is consistent consequences. A Danish social educationalist, Jens Bay, has even based a whole educational theory around it. For many parents the concept of consistency has become an established truth: if your child does not behave, it is probably because you are not being consistent enough. Several TV series about how best to rear children have been shot where consistent consequential educational methods are in the limelight, among others *Super Nanny*.

I have never been a consistent parent. My children have had different, individual rules, and these have been flexible and been adjusted to what is possible and practical. And that has not been a problem. I have talked to other parents of children without functional disorders and they often have the same experiences as I do. The parents who have talked to me most about consistent consequences are those who have children with neuropsychiatric problems. These parents have been much more consistent with those children, without it bringing a problem-free life.

What made me question the relevance of the concept of consistent consequences in ordinary rearing and not the least in social care work was two events.

First, in the TV series *Super Nanny*, one show was about a small boy, Kevin. Kevin used to kick and hit his mother at every demand or attempt at correcting his behaviour. He screamed and called her four-letter words. The family got help from a Super Nanny who introduced two new methods:

- If Kevin was angry or upset in another way, his mother was not to tell him off, but to try to make him ease off by doing breathing exercises with him.

- After that she was to bring him to the kitchen where they in cooperation would decide what consequence his agitation should be, most often less time to play video games.

The breathing exercises worked really well. Kevin calmed down in record time and stopped shouting, saying bad words, hitting and kicking. After that he went to the kitchen with his mother to decide what the consequence should be, which made him repeat that the punishment was unfair, and he once again started to hit and kick. Consequently, first a good method was used and then a lousy method that gave the opposite effect instead.

Second, a youth correctional facility I had done some diagnostic assessments for had for a few years worked with clear consequences: if you refused a demand or had an affective outburst, some privileges were withdrawn. These could be the video game, DVD or stereo being taken away from the room, the TV withdrawn, or privileges like access to cigarettes, etc. removed. We discovered that if a consequence had been triggered, a chain reaction was often started in a quickly escalating spiral. Furthermore, the person who had lost his or her privileges was angry with the staff, thought it was unfair and often brought other youths with them in a resistance against the staff. The consequence of the triggering of the consequences was that the educational work was wrecked.

I therefore decided to try to understand why so many people advocate consistent consequences as an educational or care method. I found three different schools:

- Jens Bay's educational theory of consequence. His methods were developed for working with youths with addictions and tell us that if a service-user knows the consequence of a certain behaviour, the choice of behaviour will fundamentally be a choice of consequence. If you know that you will have to quit school if you smoke marihuana this means that if you still do it, it is because you want to quit school.[*]

- Psychodynamic methods whose premise is that challenging behaviour is the consequence of attachment problems such that the service-users cannot relate to the staff at once. According to this approach, if a member of staff makes a demand on a service-user and the service-user refuses or does not meet the demand in another way, you must insist on the demand until the service-user meets it. Then predictability and clarity are created in the service-user's life and thus the attachment disorder is compensated. The service-user feels safe and secure knowing that the staff shoulder the responsibility for his or her daily life.

---

[*]   Bay 2006.

Furthermore, another aspect is added: if the service-user refuses, the staff must insist on the demand until the service-user gives up, often in an emotional outburst, which is considered something good. The service-user experiences catharsis and comes out of the crisis enriched and grown.[*]

- Educating methods with no theory. The methods directed at new parents are described in a large number of books on how to bring up children. Those who use consequence for this reason explain that if a child does something wrong and there is a clear consequence for his or her action, he or she probably chooses another behaviour next time. The argument often is: 'Then he'll learn!'

We will soon deal with Jens Bay's consequence pedagogy. To do so we must know more about how people make choices in daily life. The other two schools we can deal with at once.

The psychodynamic theorists set out from the idea that consequences bring predictability, which is considered an entirely positive word. I am not absolutely certain that is the case. That requires that a consequence is predictable to the service-user, not only to the staff or the parents. It is not certain that the service-user experiences a relation between his or her behaviour and the consequence. We can therefore use the same argument regarding psychodynamics as non-theoretical upbringing.

When children are very young they love toys with an obvious cause-and-effect function. Children play with rattles, Jack-in-the-boxes and toy phones that ring. When they are about one year old they find the light switch in the sitting room. Then they start to play with the switch. Up – there is light, down – the lights are turned off, up – there is light, down – the lights are turned off.

What is interesting about this activity is that the child can make an impact on the world around him or her from a distance. The toys the child has used previously were about making an impact on the surrounding world from a small perspective, but suddenly it can be done from a distance. The child turns the lights on and off many times before he or she is satisfied. A British study showed that a

---

[*]   Claësson and Idorn 2005.

child turns on and off the lights 600–800 times no matter whether they are allowed to or not. It has become a good way of developing an understanding of cause and effect. It might be that we as parents delay the child's development if we stop this.

After the discovery of the light switch the child looks for other causes and effects from the same point of view: how can I change the world around me in a predictable way? Children look for buttons everywhere; they explore causal effects in the social field, etc. After a couple of years the stop button in the bus is a real attraction: I can decide when a big bus with many grown-ups will stop. It is a feeling of power and possibility to change the surrounding world.

The problem with the stop button is that sometimes somebody else pushes it first. That experience can be really frightening for some children: other people can decide when a bus I am in will stop. Other people have an influence on my life. It is not only I who can make changes in predictable ways; other people can make changes that affect me in a predictable way.

The child now begins to look for this new kind of causal effect. He or she begins to ask about different things: 'Why do I have pink shoes?' 'Why do I have red hair?' 'Why are we having fish today?' To begin with the questions are asked without a context, but after a while they are more and more relevant to the child's daily life. At the age of seven the child stops asking. He or she has discovered that adults do not know everything and furthermore, that you can figure things out yourself. The child has become actively creating meaning in daily life, something that was described by Jean Piaget already 100 years ago.

At the age of 12 the child has made the world come together in a way to allow him or her to understand complex causal effects with no relation to him- or herself, for example why rubbish should not be thrown in the environment or why traffic regulations should be followed. Later development is mostly about the level of understanding of abstractions, and about widening the perspective further out into the world. This understanding is called *central coherence*.

Some children do not develop these skills in the same way. I have worked with people with autism who still at the age of 36 think it is interesting to turn on and off the lights. I have also worked with a great number of children of average intelligence who have not developed a good understanding of causes and effects.

> **Kirsten** is 36 years old and has ADHD. She lives in her own flat and is assisted by a carer from the municipality to make her daily life work. She has difficulties making plans and managing her finances and to fit cleaning into her schedule, etc.
>
> Kirsten's door leads to a small garden-patch. She tells me: 'I'm always a bit worried when I'm going out. I'm not absolutely sure I'll come to my own garden.'

Kirsten's understanding of causes and effects is so poor she has difficulties using it to predict consequences. She has walked out the door several times a day for years, but is still not sure she will come to the same garden every time. She admits that it is crazy and that she rationally can predict that her garden has not moved, but the little emotional insecurity is still there.

> **Roy** is 14 years old. He has no formal diagnosis, but has always had behaviour problems. One day a teacher enters the classroom and says: 'Time for maths.' After a while the teacher asks Roy why he haven't got his maths book open. Roy says: 'You never said I should take out my maths book.' Roy has had four maths lessons every week for seven years, but he never understood that in every maths lesson you use the maths book.

People with problems in this field are not actively creating meaning from Piaget's point of view. He noticed that his children tried to find causal explanations in daily life all the time, and described that. From that we understand that his children did not have any neuropsychiatric disorders and no intellectual disabilities. The people I meet in my clinical work are definitely not actively creating meaning. They don't discover causes and effects other people see at once, and for that reason have great difficulties in daily life.

If you do not try to find causal effects in your childhood, you do not develop *an understanding of contexts*, which leads to your having difficulties predicting the future on the whole. People use understanding of complex relations so as to be prepared for different consequences of events and behaviours. This means that we often are quite prepared for the consequences of our actions. If you do not have that understanding you are not prepared in situations other people easily would have predicted.

> **Simon** is 17 years old and has Asperger's syndrome and has a special interest in Arsenal Football Club. He has a lot of Arsenal stuff, everything from shirts, scarves, flags to game plans. He sees almost all home matches and some away matches.
>
> When there is a new shirt in store he naturally wants it and asks his mother if he can have £40. She says no because she thinks he has enough paraphernalia already. Simon only sees one way out of the situation: he takes his soft air gun and goes to the closest supermarket and threatens the check-out assistant to get the day's cash. He gets about £1000, takes £40 and returns the rest. Then he runs away.
>
> One of the customers in the supermarket runs after him. Simon does not pay attention to that, but only runs for 300 yards. Then he starts to walk slowly and calmly. The customer catches up with him, grabs a board that lies on the ground and hits him on the head. Simon falls and the customer sits on top of him and calls the police.
>
> I talk to Simon a few weeks later. He says: 'What had I done to him? He had nothing to do with that. I don't want to be here (in a youth correctional facility), I didn't do anything violent. I only took £40. The lady got the rest back.'

Simon has several problems in this situation. He performs the robbery without considering what the consequences might be. He is clearly surprised that he is now in a youth correctional facility. Moreover he had not foreseen that other people could react to his behaviour. It was a total surprise to him that the customer was going after him.

In Simon's life this event is not out of the ordinary. He has had a number of conflicts in his life because he has not been able to relate to other people's responses to his behaviour. He is surprised that other people hit back and cannot understand why his friends do not want to be with him when they have been in a fight. Many things that are predictable to other people are surprising to him.

Asperger's syndrome and other autism spectrum disorders mean that you have difficulties predicting the future at all. For some people to such a degree that a clear structure in daily life is needed, which is the basis for the structure-based autism pedagogy Treatment and Education of Autistic and related Communication handicapped CHildren (TEACCH). People with autism, however, are not really more dependent on structure than other people and may even cheat the structure.

> **Axel** is 42 years old and has autism. He has very limited language. He lives in a group home and has staff nearby 24/7. Axel is totally dependent on a schedule, and with a good schedule he manages daily life, including his hygiene, cleaning of the group home and 24 hours rhythm.
>
> Axel likes coffee. Every day he tries to put more coffee pictograms on his schedule.

Axel does not need a structure for the sake of the structure, which he even tries to cheat. He has a need of structure because it also means an exclusion of possible events. Axel cannot predict the future and gets into a state of anxiety if he does not know what is going to happen, but when he has his schedule he feels safe and secure. Nothing unpredictable will happen.

Psychodynamic consequential thinking is founded on a consistent adult assisting the child's predictability in daily life. In practice this means that if an adult has made a demand, it must be carried through no matter what the child's response to it is. In the long run it is believed that this will ensure that the child gains security in the adult's responsibility for the situation, which can be the foundation for the building of relationships. The greater the problems, the greater consistency may be needed.

If the child has not developed an understanding of contexts many of the adults' demands will come as a surprise. If the adults then stick to their demands only because the demand has been made, the child will unfortunately not experience more predictability in daily life. It will only mean unpredictable demands on complete submission. This if something does not lead to security, but violent insecurity. Some psychodynamic psychologists think this insecurity is something good, as catharsis is then reached. That concept we have already discussed and discarded. Instead we can use another principle:

It is never too late to give up!

Sometimes we will make too great demands by mistake. I once told my children: 'If you don't stop fighting, there won't be any Christmas gifts!' Of course I did not carry it through in reality. That would have been a direct assault and would not have improved the relationship with my children. Educational and care staff sometimes act on the same principle: in the bus: 'If you're not quiet and stop fighting, we won't go on the excursion, but home!' If the children do not stop fighting perhaps you go home instead of going on the excursion. Is that good learning? Do the children consider that a fair consequence?

I have a principle: if the child thinks it is unfair and a punishment, then that is probably the case. I can try to explain it away as much as I like; I still cannot change the child's experience, and the child will not gain trust in me because of my consistent reasoning. The pedagogical truth is in the service-user's experience, not in the staff's or the parents' reasoning.

Daniel started school at a normal age. Until then he had been at home with his mother. It soon turned out that he had amazing skills in chair throwing. At every setback he reacted violently, and he threw furniture almost every day. After a couple of weeks he had to quit school, and it was decided that he would start school next year instead, at a special unit.

Next year he started school again, but his behaviour had not improved. He reacted violently in demanding situations and when he experienced something as being unfair. He had great learning difficulties and did not learn to read, write or count in the three years he went to the special unit. He did however improve his strength and was more violent in situations of conflict.

After three years his time at the special unit was ended and he was going to continue his studies in regular school. He was placed in a mainstream school. That was not very wise. He spent a lot of time outside the classroom, he left school, and he still threw furniture at times. After a few months he was as usual sent out of the classroom, whereupon he threw in a big cracker among the children and ran off. He was not welcome back to the school.

The local authorities did not know what to do. Daniel's mother was not interested in him ending up in a childcare facility, but wanted the authorities to find a school suited for his needs. Eventually it was agreed that he was to try him in a special school for children with intellectual disabilities. It was not believed that he had a learning disability, but he had not acquired any skills or knowledge in school.

Daniel tells us: 'After a couple of days we had PE. We were going to play football, and it was great fun. Then I tackled a boy hard and the teacher gave me a red card. I was really upset and felt that it was starting all over again; my head boiled and I was about to run amok. The teacher looked at me and said: "Was that too much for you? Do you want us to go to the teachers' staff room – I have some cream buns there?" I was really surprised. Nobody had tried that before. A teacher that could see it was hard for me. We left to have cream buns.'

Daniel says that from that day he sometimes would go for a walk when something was too difficult for him, sometimes he walked with a teacher and bought coke and sometimes they sat down and talked. Daniel no longer threw furniture. After a couple of years he learnt to read and count and today, when he is 24 years old, he studies law at university. He has the diagnoses ADHD and atypical autism.

He calls the pedagogy that saved him 'coke pedagogy' and says that the teacher seeing him and understanding that he could not meet the demand made him gain trust in a teacher for the first time.

Had the teachers continued to be consistent and hard we would probably have a criminal young man instead of a future lawyer. Daniel reckons that the teacher saved his life.

Consequence and structure

When consequence is questioned some people are upset and say: 'Should we completely ignore what the service-user does and let everything pass by?' No, of course we should not do that. But we must differentiate between structure and consequence. Often we believe that structure is good and then we must have consequences to motivate the service-user to be a part of the structure. That is how we think about ordinary children, and it is possible it works with them. In the field of special needs that is, however, not true.

Structure is good, that is true. It helps the service-user compensate for a poor central coherence and creates predictability and security. The best thing is that many of our service-users like structure. They do not need to be motivated by threats of consequences and they are happy to be part of different structures, if those structures are adjusted to each individual service-user.

Threats of consequences may also sometimes work. There may be service-users who want to know what will happen if they do not stick to the structure. To them the threat of consequences is a part of the structure, and may be something they have learnt through poor pedagogy. Therefore, it may in exceptional cases have an effect to say: 'If you're not quiet we won't go on the excursion, but home again.' The children may then fall silent, at least for 30 seconds.

The problem arises when the threat is realized. Then the service-user often thinks the consequence is unfair and unpredictable. Then trust of staff or parent is reduced, and consequently the ability to be a part of the structure in the future. The ability to keep one's self-control is immediately reduced.

We must simply rely on the wish to be a part of the structure and on our ability to maintain the structures even when it is difficult. We cannot let the structure depend on the threat of an intervention we would rather avoid, especially if the intervention in the long run diminishes trust in the relationship.

If consequence is used from the point of view that the service-user will probably learn when the consequence is unpleasant, it is rather a punishing method. We know that punishment does not have the desired effect. To change the name to consequence does not mean the effect will improve. When I hear staff or parents say 'Then he might learn', I usually say that it is probably a sign of someone having great difficulties learning, just as the sentence 'That can't be true' often means that it is.

However, to give in is not a good general educational method. Every time you give in you must immediately find a way to avoid doing so the next time you are in a similar situation. That is done either by estimating the risks or by introducing another educational method.

> **Harry** is six years old and has a moderate intellectual disability. He is at a fair with his mother and sees a small horse he really wants. He asks to have it, but his mother says no. Harry starts crying and screaming out loud. The mother immediately buys the horse and Harry stops screaming.

Harry's mother cannot trust herself always to be able to manage a situation by buying what he asks for. Next time he might want a live horse. She must assess the event and make a plan of action. At first she estimates why everything became so hard for him. Harry was stressed by the noisy environment at the fair and his surplus was consequently lower than usual. Furthermore, she had not talked to him about the fact that he could not buy anything, The risk of the arousal of such a situation was therefore greater than normally.

The action plan can therefore take several forms:

- In the future we avoid bringing Harry to the fair.

- Next time Harry is going to a fair we will talk to him about the fact that he cannot buy anything.

- Next time Harry is going to the fair we tell him that he can have a bag of sweets if he manages not to scream if he sees something he wants.

All these three possible action plans entail that we will not have to give in next time. They have clear educational focuses. And they do not require that Harry takes responsibility. To make up an action plan is to take the educational responsibility.

Rationality and 'on purpose' behaviour

A common misunderstanding is that people have far-sighted control of their behaviour. We often believe that you choose your behaviour from an analysis of pros and cons of different behaviours. Behaviour is in this way deliberate, and 'on purpose'. This means that we are annoyed by behaviours we think our fellow-beings could have chosen not to do. This in turn means that consequence can be used as a method to teach man to choose right.

Different philosophers have contributed to this misunderstanding. The 18th-century philosopher Immanuel Kant said that people were responsible for their choices, and therefore should be punished when choosing wrong. In that way people would be helped to choose correctly. The Danish philosopher Søren Kierkegaard did not agree. He lived 100 years after Kant and did not believe that man was such a rational creature, and instead asserted that *Life is understood backwards, but must be lived forwards.*

By this he meant that we do not act far-sightedly with control, but that we act on our gut feeling. Afterwards, when we look over our shoulder, we may understand why we did as we did. He also complained about himself never having the time to look over his shoulder, and therefore often did not know why he had acted as he had.[*]

The active choice keeps coming back in the thinking of other philosophers. It is prevalent in Descartes' thinking. He believed that people are rational creatures and therefore choose almost like a computer by thinking and estimating the consequences of different behaviours. Kant developed this further and in the 1960s Sartre argued that people actively choose their life and their behaviour, and therefore always have a personal responsibility for their behaviour. As I have already noted, the Danish social worker Jens Bay has developed this thinking into a method he calls consequence pedagogy, which in short says that if the service-user knows the consequence of his or her behaviour, he or she will actively choose the consequence if she chooses the behaviour. This is helped by making the consequences plain and making sure that they are carried through. The method is mainly used in the care of addicts in Denmark, but it has influenced the Danish educational debate for decades, just as it is the foundation of a part of the methadone treatment in Sweden.

Internationally, among others, the American doctor and philosopher Antonio Damasio has shown that Søren Kierkegaard

---

[*]   Kierkegaard 1843.

was not all wrong. Damasio has shown that people choose by using their feelings.

Whenever you are faced with a difficult choice, not only information on how you choose, but also the associated feeling is saved in the brain. In new situations the memory is scanned for situations that are reminiscent of the new situation, and you choose according to the way that has brought the most positive emotions before. The emotional life in Damasio's thinking is the basis for behavioural choices and therefore a function of survival. Damasio believes that most choices are unconscious, just like Søren Kierkegaard argued. The difference is that Damasio does not mean that in retrospect you always understand why you acted as you did.*

Some scholars at the University of Lund, Sweden, have researched this in more detail. Young men were shown photos of young women, two at a time, and asked to choose which of them was the prettiest. When they had chosen, they were shown the picture they had picked and were asked why. The men always had an explanation; it could be the beautiful hair or the stunning eyes.

However, in some of these choices, the photo of the woman they had not picked as the most beautiful was shown. The research leader had two pictures in each hand, one of them hidden, and like a conjurer he showed the other photo. He still asked why the man had chosen this very woman. It turned out that the men still gave good explanations for their choices, even though they had actually chosen the direct opposite. This tells us that the men did not know why they had chosen as they had. Choosing and explaining can therefore be seen as two completely separate functions. When we choose we have no conscious ulterior motive, and when we explain it, it is an explanation that is based on how we see that we have chosen.**

One school in psychology, narrative psychology, has also looked at how we understand or explain our behaviour. The advocates of this school reckon that people often explain their behaviour in relation to its outcome. It is believed that elderly people describe their lives from their mood: when they are happy, they describe their lives as good lives filled with joy; when they are sad, they describe

---

*   Damasio 1994.

**   Johansson *et al.* 2007.

their lives as hard and filled with sorrow. How the lives have actually been is not that important; you choose from your memories and put them together in different cause-and-effect contexts according to the mood at the time.

If we put these two factors together we get an updated Kierkegaard sentence:

You act forwards and explain backwards.

This means that we choose with our feelings without thinking too consciously, and when we afterwards try to understand why, we are happy with an explanation that renders meaning to the situation we are in then. We will take a couple of examples. The great decisions in life are often made without us thinking them over that much. When we pick a life companion we often do it on the run, without estimating the consequences in the long run. Few people have sat down and made lists of pros and cons of the different candidates. The choice of life companion is generally considered an emotional choice. Buying a place to live is a completely different matter. The estate agents and the banks sell it as one of the most important choices in life. Most of us believe that we buy a place to live with our brain and not our heart. Damasio and experience, however, tell us differently.

When my partner and I were buying a house together for the first time we had quite high demands. We wanted a smaller house, preferably old, that was situated near the sea. We looked at many houses, and eventually chose a small, ugly house near the sea in a small community north of the Swedish city Malmö. The house is in a street lined with beautiful old houses built of local brick facing the street. When one of our daughters had been there taking a look at it before we moved in she asked us: 'Why have you bought the ugliest house in the street? So many beautiful houses, and you have bought the ugly one.' Our house was renovated in the 1970s and the previous owners had put up a brick facing in an, at the time, up-to-date fashion, changed the size of the windows and tiled an asbestos cement sheeting roof. The house looks like a small house from the 1970s in the middle of a street of old houses. When people ask us today why we bought that particular house we say: 'It was the location that settled the matter.' We do not know for sure, but it seems to be a good explanation, and people seem to buy it. What we know is that this was the house we felt best about buying.

Estate agents style houses and flats and sell them faster and more expensively. A house is sold faster if it smells of fresh cinnamon buns. Why is that so? Because we choose with our heart, not our brain. We choose what feels good. And that is a good way of choosing.

Phineas Gage is a classic case study in brain research. Phineas worked as a foreman in the railway construction in New England in the US in the 1840s. His job was to manage a team of explosives workers. They bored a hole in the mountain, poured gunpowder, a fuse and sand into it, and then tamped down the gunpowder before lighting the fuse.

One day when Phineas as usual took charge of the gunpowder and prepared the explosion he forgot to pour the sand. He then pushed the tamping iron into the hole to tamp down the gunpowder, but was surprised by the gunpowder exploding and sending the iron bar in through his cheek and out through the top of his head just behind the hairline.

Phineas did not lose consciousness, and at first it was believed that he had not been injured by the accident at all, except for the fact that one of his eyes had been destroyed. After he had returned to work it was however soon obvious that he could no longer choose correctly. He had lost the ability to choose with his feelings and had to rely on reason. Phineas died in a state of destitution a few years later after a life marked by impulsivity and faulty decisions.[*]

When we choose with our feelings we are far more nuanced than when we choose by estimating pros and cons of different choices. We do not have the brain capacity necessary to estimate the consequences enough to choose with our mind.

Our gut feeling may even have evolved to help us choose in a nuanced and fast way.

People with intellectual disabilities, and not the least people with neuropsychiatric difficulties, rarely develop the ability of choosing

---

[*]   Damasio 1994.

with their feelings as well as other people do. I often say that they also act forwards and explain backwards, but not as well as other people. We will look at an example:

Max is 16 years old. He lives with his little brother one year his junior and their parents in a small city in Sweden. Max goes to school, in the ninth grade. Max has no friends, but his brother has plenty. Max often tries to tag along when his brother has friends over.

One Sunday Max and his father are cleaning the garage when his father asks him: 'Isn't it about time you got a girlfriend?' Max thinks about this for the rest of the day, and decides to give it a try.

Next day, he goes to the shopping centre after school. He looks at the girls and when he has found a girl he thinks is pretty he approaches her and grabs her breasts. She screams and boxes his ears. Max runs away. He is surprised and frightened and runs all the way home.

Next day, Tuesday, he returns to the shopping centre after school. This time he looks at the girls for a longer time and eventually finds a girl he not only finds pretty, but who seems quite calm as well. She has long, black hair and she stands with a group of boys, who also are black-haired. He hears that the other boys call her Samira, which Max thinks is a beautiful name.

Max approaches her and grabs her breasts. She screams and the boys ask him what he thinks he is doing. Max does not know what to say and tries to run away. The boys catch up with him and start beating him. He falls. They kick him a few times and say: 'And now you leave our sister alone!'

Max goes home. His whole body hurts and he bleeds from the nose. His mother asks him what has happened and Max tells her he has fallen with his bike. He knows that you do not always talk to your parents about girlfriends and the like.

On Wednesday after school Max goes to the shopping centre once again. He searches a long time for a girl who looks nice and pretty and then approaches a beautiful girl. Just when he is about to grab her breasts a guard asks him: 'Hello, what are you doing? Are you the person who's been grabbing girls' breasts yesterday and the day before that?' 'Yes,' Max replies.

The girl leaves and the guard asks Max to come with him. After a while the police arrive and Max is brought to the police station.

The following day I talk to Max and ask him why he has been grabbing girls' breasts. He tells me that he tried to get a girlfriend. I ask him how he was imagining it all. What was most interesting was that on the Wednesday he thought: 'It didn't work yesterday, and not the day before. Then it'll probably work today.'

Most other boys who had tried Max's method would have thought 'That was probably not a good strategy' after the first box on the ear, and tried other methods in the future. Max did not connect the feeling of disgrace with his action, and consequently did not adjust his behaviour accordingly. Next day he did exactly the same thing, and even on the third day he was about to continue on the same track. He simply found it easier to repeat the behaviour, even though it demonstrably did not work, than find new ways to act. The technical term for this repeating of behaviours in an inflexible way is *perseveration*.

Max was diagnosed with Asperger's syndrome. His difficulties learning from his emotional experiences are however not limited to that diagnosis, but are also seen in people with intellectual disabilities, ADHD and all other neuropsychiatric diagnoses, where a tendency to repeat behaviours that clearly have not worked previously is common.

This is the first part of the updated Kierkegaard sentence. The other part is that we explain our behaviour backwards. Here people with neuropsychiatric disorders or intellectual disabilities have problems as well.

We have previously discussed difficulties with understanding contexts and the concept of *central coherence*. If you have difficulties understanding causes and effects in a larger context, it is naturally difficult to work out possible reasons for your own behaviour. Moreover, many people with neuropsychiatric difficulties or intellectual disabilities have, as a result of their poor empathic ability, difficulties estimating what other people will believe in. This means that other people do not consider many of their explanations credible and they are therefore often suspected of lying. When they are asked why they are lying they maintain that they are speaking the truth.

And they are, to the same extent as we are. I do not know if we bought our house because of its geographical position, but it is a plausible explanation and people buy it because I am good enough at understanding what people might believe in.

Therefore, on the one hand you have to understand and be able to manage unreasonable actions that are repeated, and on the other hand you must manage not to ask why; you will not get any satisfying answer anyway. And the question is whether anyone has a use for explanations at all.

The ability to use emotional experiences when faced with difficult choices is neatly illustrated by the following. Research has shown that many people with autism have larger brains than others. An acquaintance of mine, Aage Sinkbæk, has Asperger's syndrome and has written a book about his life.[*] He says: 'It's a good thing that my brain is bigger than others, considering how much thinking I must do to make the right decisions.' Aage has a very large head and notes that he finds it difficult to use his emotional experiences and therefore always must estimate the possible consequences in daily life, but that he still does not always succeed.

If, from this knowledge, we are to assess Jens Bay's consequence pedagogy, which means that you presuppose that the choice of behaviour also is a choice of consequences, we must unfortunately say that the choice for one thing is not an active choice (you live life forwards without conscious choices), but an emotional choice (which actually could be an argument for his method). Regrettably emotional choices do not work very well for people with a reduced central coherence, and that is the group most often found in care and special educational contexts. The method may therefore be useful in the upbringing of ordinary children, but it does not work in the fields of care and special education. And with that we should have killed the concept of consequence completely.

Reward pedagogy and bribes

When we now have killed off consequential thinking in special education, we have a problem. Can we no longer use rewards? We will look at rewards for two reasons:

---

[*]   Sinkbæk 2002.

- It is a widely used educational tool that many pedagogues have had great use of. A great part of the cognitive behaviour therapy methods have proven effective in many scientific studies. It ought to work!

- We harbour a great fear of rewarding negative behaviour. Should we put that fear aside?

Reward pedagogy springs from behaviourism which, very simplified, sets out from strengthening behaviour by relating behaviour to a pleasant event, for example giving sweets to children who have done their homework. The children will love to do their homework as they connect homework with sweets. I am not going to challenge the foundation of behaviourism, but look at what we actually do when we work with rewards.

> **Mike** is 12 years old. He lives with his mother and goes to school at a special school unit. He has started to spit on people in the street on his way to school. He thinks it is hilarious; people react so differently when they are spat at.
>
> Mike's teacher does not like this and when Mike spits at an elderly man when the class is in town, the teacher decides to deal with it. They work with the conversation tool Cat-kit, and after a couple of weeks they give it a try: Mike and his teacher Steve go for a long walk. When they are back in school Steve says: 'How good of you, Mike, not to spit on anybody. I think that is really good. What do you think?' Mike thinks it was a bit hard, but 'they may be sad if I spit at them'. 'That's good,' Steve says, 'now I think we should sit down and have a cup of cocoa together.'
>
> After a while I enter the room. I see them having cocoa and says: 'How lucky you are, Mike. Why are you having cocoa?'
>
> 'I don't know,' Mike replies, 'I think Steve was thirsty.'

This little story is interesting from several points of view. Most 12-year-olds would no doubt know that the cocoa was either a reward or a celebration of the fact that Mike had not spat on anybody during the walk. They would use their ability of actively creating meaning and reach that conclusion. Accordingly, the cocoa would be an educational effort that could help Mike's further development.

However, Mike has a reduced central coherence and consequently has difficulties seeing relations between causes and effects. He does not look for connections in daily life, and all relations must therefore be explicitly explained to him. This means that Mike does not see many of the small rewards he is given by people around him in the form of smiles, praise and other positive contact. This may also be a partial reason for his having developed a challenging behaviour.

The story of Mike and the cocoa is interesting from another point of view as well. As Mike does not see the connection between the praise and the cocoa, we cannot expect him to see connections between negative behaviour and possible positive consequences either. A common misunderstanding is that positive diversions should be avoided to ensure that negative behaviour is not rewarded and consequently is strengthened.

If you wish to work with rewards in the fields of care or special education some fundamental conditions must be met:

- The connection must be explained thoroughly, for example by, in the case of Mike, telling him that he is getting cocoa *because* he did not spit at anybody.

- You must make sure that the reward is given immediately after the behaviour you want to reward.[*]

These conditions are often met in school through different reward systems where you are immediately given a token (in a token economy) or a gold star when you have done something correctly. It is actually quite comical that the behaviourists have discovered that rewards in the normal group are less efficient if the person knows why he or she is rewarded whereas it is the other way round in the field of special education. It makes me wonder whether the token economy is a behaviourist method at all.

I actually do not believe that reward systems in the fields of care and special education are about rewards in the proper behaviouristic sense, but rather about bribes and wages. That does not make them

---

[*]   LaVigna and Willis 2002.

less effective or good, but moves our understanding to something that, to me, is more equal.

My work involves, among other things, giving lectures, which entails quite some travelling and days away from home. It does not matter that much as long as they are on weekdays. I do however like to be at home at the weekends because my partner Susan is off then and I enjoy spending time with her. The Saturday morning should preferably be spent sitting in the kitchen or in the garden solving crosswords together.

Sometimes I am contacted by people who want me to give a lecture on a Saturday as it is not possible on weekdays. Then I am faced with a problem. I do like to give a lecture, but they cannot listen to me on weekdays and I do not really want to work weekends.

I have solved this in a simple way: I ask for a 50 per cent extra fee. Then I am motivated to give a lecture even on a Saturday, and at the same time limit the number of Saturdays I have to work; I am too expensive for some, so they solve the problem so I can come on a weekday instead.

Our service-users may feel the same way. They may find it hard to carry through certain activities or manage to restrain themselves from certain behaviours, unless they feel it is worth it. And if you have difficulties with causes and effects it is not certain that you can see it is worth it without a small bribe to make the value clear. Therefore we will use bribes in a smart way:

- What bribe will motivate this specific service-user?
- How can I make clear to the service-user that the bribe is a motivator?
- How can I make sure the bribe is immediate?
- How can I make clear the connection between the bribe and the behaviour I want?

Alex is 14 years old. Apart from a slight learning disability and Asperger's syndrome he has a physical illness, Ehlers-Danloss syndrome, which among other things means that he is in great pain. One of the consequences of the illness is that he must wear specially made shoes. Alex does however not like to go to the shoemakers, mostly because the shoes hurt before they fit really well.

His parents have come up with a good way to motivate him to go to the shoemakers. His mother says: 'Come on, Alex, we're going to the shoemakers now, and you'll get a coke in the car.' Alex likes coke so he happily enters the car. While at the shoemakers his mother says: 'Let's go to the shoemakers now and when we're finished, there is a coke for you in the glove compartment.' Alex is in this way motivated to cooperate with the visit to the shoemakers.

After a couple of years his mother thinks it works fairly well. She therefore unconsciously increases the stake. On their way home from the shoemakers one time she says: 'We must go to the hypermarket on our way home so we can eat on time.' Alex counters: 'Then I think I must have one of the Lego castles they have for £120.' His mother thinks they should rather go home in that case. She will do the shopping later. Alex is pleased, but his mother is slightly frustrated.

She therefore calls me in the evening and asks: 'You said it was OK with bribes and that two cokes could pull Alex all the way through the visit to the shoemakers. Today I wanted to bring him to the hypermarket as well and then inflation had struck. He wanted a Lego castle worth £120.'

As a matter of fact Alex's behaviour is amazing. He has been motivated with a coke or two to take part in difficult situations. The demand to go to the hypermarket would perhaps only have cost one coke on an ordinary day, but his mother made the demand on one of the worst days there are, shoemaker day. Alex estimated how hard it would be to go to the hypermarket this specific day, and found that he probably could be motivated if he got a Lego castle.

He has developed the ability to estimate how he can be motivated. I think this is a great development and an amazing skill in his life. He has Asperger's syndrome and therefore does not do anything to make other people happy or to be a part of the community, he has difficulties estimating those effects and cannot see its worth, but he can be motivated, and now he can estimate how hard it is and what it will cost. This corresponds to how I raise my fee on Saturdays.

Fear of rewarding negative behaviour

I don't think it is that easy to reward and consequently strengthen negative behaviour in people with an intellectual disability or neuropsychiatric disorders. If it were that easy, we could probably also reward and strengthen positive behaviour, and then we would probably not have many service-users with challenging behaviour. To explain this we will look at the story about Victor, told by Andy McDonnell.

> **Victor** is ten years old and has an intellectual disability and autism. He is interested in animals, sea lions in particular. One day he is at the zoo with two teachers and three friends. At 11:30 they go to the sea lion cage to see the animals being fed. It is the absolute climax of the excursion. The sea lions are trained in different tricks and jump through hoops, play with balls and the like. After every trick they are given half a herring. Victor is overjoyed; he jumps back and forth and makes loud sounds of joy. After about 20 minutes the keeper turns the bucket upside down and says: 'Now there is no more food. The sea lions will be fed again at two o'clock.'
>
> Victor is happy at first. He does not really know the time so he remains standing waiting for the sea lions to be fed again.

In this situation the teachers have different alternatives:

- They can stay with all four pupils. It would not be easy; none of the children is good at waiting.

- They could split: one teacher leaves with the other three children and one stays with Victor. Unfortunately, Victor finds waiting very hard and he would soon start to react negatively.

- They could pull Victor away, perhaps by grabbing his wrist and pretend that they were holding hands. This could result in Victor starting to scream and kick.

- They could say: 'Let's all go and have some ice cream.'

Victor loves ice cream more than sea lions, so the last suggestion would solve the situation. However, it is hard for many people to do so as they think they would then reward his negative behaviour. There would be a risk that he wants an ice cream before he can leave the lion cages, another before he can leave the elephant house and perhaps another one before he can leave the zoo. There is even a risk that the teachers cannot make him work in school next day without using ice creams.

I believe this risk is non-existent and is only in our minds. Andy McDonnell has denoted this the result of the thinking disorder *catastrophe thinking*. If we could reward Victor's negative behaviour this easily, we could reward his positive behaviour just as easily and then we would not have those problems we do in daily life.[*]

There is no reason to be afraid to encourage negative behaviour by diversions in pupils with retardation or neuropsychiatric disorders. It is not that simple. On the other hand, there are plenty of ways to use diversions to avoid challenging behaviour, if we only dare take the risk. We will return to this later on in the book.

Conceptions of the causes of behaviour

Motives

Many of our basic ideas about why different service-users have different behaviours have their origin in our power of insight. When we see a certain behaviour we think: 'If it were me having that behaviour, why would I have it?'

Power of insight is not a bad quality in educational work, but you must always remember that when you work with people defined as being in need of special assistance, you work with people with different qualifications from you.

> **Peter** is sentenced for attempted murder. As a 19-year-old he had his own flat with personal assistants who would help him in daily life. Peter has the diagnosis of Asperger's syndrome.
>
> The staff at Peter's home had certain rules that Peter should follow. The rules were agreed upon with Peter's mother. He could not drink alcohol and he could not play computer games

---

[*]   McDonnell, Waters and Jones 2002.

for more than two hours a day. He had to keep to time and had a fairly strict structure for his daily life.

One day Peter was angry. For some time he had been vexed about not being allowed to play computer games for more than two hours a day and had had a few confrontations with the staff. One staff member in particular had persisted in this rule and made clear that there was nothing Peter could do to change this fact. Therefore one night Peter entered the staff room and tried to strangle the assistant. Luckily enough, Peter is a weak boy so the assistant could get free and call the police.

Peter was sentenced to forensic psychiatric care with the prospect of being placed in a group home with the target group youths with Asperger's syndrome and challenging behaviour.

At first he was placed in a closed psychiatric ward. After that the idea was that he was to be moved as soon as a relevant group home for him was found. However, Peter was tremendously bored in the psychiatric ward. It was always quiet, except for when a patient ran amok, and Peter was always silenced when he tried to get some life into the ward. The other patients were in a very poor state when they arrived at the ward, but as soon as they were feeling better they were moved to an open ward.

Peter has a heightened pain threshold. That is not unusual for people with neuropsychiatric disorders. In the case of Peter it means that he sometimes does things other people find challenging. When he was bored at the ward he could sit tearing his nails off. According to him it did not hurt at all. This however led to him not being moved to a group home as he was believed to be in need of further psychiatric care. The staff were thinking: 'How bad would I feel, if I had to tear my nails off to endure life?'

Our power of insight means that we put ourselves in the service-user's place and think just that: 'If that were me doing so, why would I do it?'

We will take a few examples. They will help us correct our perception of reality. We do not work with people like ourselves, but with people with completely different prerequisites.

Sofie is 10 years old. She has Asperger's syndrome and is integrated in a mainstream school. Her school is situated in the country and has a total of 80 pupils. Sofie has difficulties relating to other people's actions. She remains seated when the rest of the pupils leave the classroom unless she knows where they are going. The staff have worked with this and now she leaves the room when the other pupils do. She does however not always go in the same direction. Once she called home and asked where her mother was; she was standing by herself waiting to be picked up from school. It was 10am and everybody had left the classroom to go to handicraft. Sofie had seen them leave, but had gone to the road to wait for her mother. The mother had to tell her she had handicraft now and should go to the handicraft room.

One day Sofie was suddenly alone in the classroom as so many times before. She went outside to find her classmates and found them standing in a long line with the rest of the pupils of the school. At the front a couple of teachers were standing helping five pupils fry pancakes over a fire.

Sofie went to her friend Peter who was standing with a frying pan with a long handle with an almost ready pancake. She took a plate and a fork, took the pancake from his pan and said politely: 'Thank you very much, Peter' and sat down to eat.

Sofie's teacher talked to Sofie's mother the same afternoon and asked: 'And what do you think Sofie wanted to accomplish by jumping the queue?' Sofie's mother replied: 'She probably wanted a pancake.'

Sofie does not understand why her friends do certain things. She has written a book on this that has been published in Denmark, Sweden and England. It is called *Do You Understand Me?*[*] In this specific case she did not understand why all the children were standing in a long line. She did not make the connection between the fire, the pancakes and the long line of children. She says: 'My classmates do so many strange things.'

The teacher quickly applied a motive to Sofie's action, that she would have had herself if she had had the same behaviour: Sofie

---

[*]   Brøsen 2008.

wanted to provoke and manipulate. That was not the case as Sofie's behaviour often is quite simple.

In the case of Sofie and of many others with neuropsychiatric disorders this principle is true:

The motive is closer to the act than we think.

This entails quite a high degree of empathy from us if we are to work out a person's motives. We cannot turn to ourselves because we have a far too good understanding of causes and effects, and of how our actions affect other people.

Then there are people who, despite neuropsychiatric problems or mental retardation, do try to manipulate. My experience is that this is one of the most provoking things there are for staff and parents. When this comes up in guidance I normally ask: 'How long has it been since you yourself manipulated?' It turns out that most often if it was not today or yesterday it was at least last week. If educational or care staff refuse to admit they have manipulated, I am suspicious. Is that not exactly what you are paid to do? To make the service-user behave in a certain way by using different methods?

I think that what provokes the staff is that the service-user is such a poor manipulator. A good manipulation is when both the person manipulating and the person who has been manipulated are happy and the manipulation is not discovered. Our service-users fail to do so.

> **Christina** has autism. She is 48 years old and lives in a group home with two other service-users. Christina likes to know the working rota of the staff, so she knows in advance who will work with her. If a member of staff is ill and the rota consequently is not true she is very upset. This has been solved by her not knowing their working rota in advance, which has given her a much calmer daily life.
>
> She does however try to find out who will be working, which makes the staff tell her: 'We won't talk more about the rota today. You'll see it'll work out just fine.'
>
> One day Christina does not think that is enough and asks: 'Who will cook on Friday?' This is a way of manipulating to get

the wanted information. It is however very obvious that it is a manipulation and the staff do not buy it.

Another time she really wants to go out for dinner and tells a member of staff: 'On Friday we're going for dinner at a restaurant.' The member of staff then asks her who she has settled that with, which Christina answers with 'I'll settle that with Eva tomorrow.' Again an attempt at manipulation, but once again a very clumsy attempt.

If we are provoked by these attempts it cannot be because she tries to manipulate us, because we all do, but it must be because she does it so poorly.

To manipulate well you must be able to put yourself in other people's ways of thinking. You have to be able to predict the other person's reaction and what behaviour it will trigger. If you do not have sufficient empathic ability you will not succeed in doing so and the manipulation will be very poor.

Lying works the same way. A parent asked me why her son with ADHD lied so much. I asked how much he lied and she told me it was several times a week. The son was 14 years old. I do not know if you remember what it was like to be 14 years old. I know that I lied quite a lot, and psychoanalysts believe there are good reasons to lie in your teens when you are developing your identity and are distinguishing yourself from other people.[*]

It must be nearly impossible to lie as much as other 14-year-olds when you have ADHD. To succeed in doing so you must be good at lying and knowing what the other person knows or can work out. That simply requires a good empathic ability. Unfortunately, you rarely have that when you have ADHD, and even more rarely in autism spectrum disorders or intellectual disabilities, so it is not strange that the lies are discovered.

I think that a reasonable lie or attempt at manipulation by a person with a neuropsychiatric disorder should be rewarded; it is after all an attempt to use empathic ability. I often say: 'You, if you're going to manipulate me you should do it better, for example by...'

---

[*]   Tosone 2003.

and then give a good example. In that way we also might develop the person's empathy.

Motivation

When working with people with neuropsychiatric problems you often encounter the idea that a service-user is unmotivated. The staff may say that it is hard to work with him, because he is unmotivated for changes. A pupil in special school is unmotivated to learn and skip classes a lot, and an addicted teenager with ADHD may be unmotivated for treatment.

Of course a lack of motivation is a problem for staff or parents. However, it is not necessarily a problem for the service-user. Often the lack of motivation is a way to deal with demands; if I am motivated I must participate and then I will be put under stress. In other cases a lack of motivation is the result of having failed so many times there is no use taking an active part.

If you as a member of staff feel powerless you may, as has already been discussed, throw the blame on somebody else. The problem with blaming other people is that you then lose the possibility of exerting an influence and lose even more power in relation to the educational or care work. We have discussed blaming parents, but you may just as often blame service-users themselves. One way is to blame their motivation.

It is problematic to blame a service-user's deficient development on lack of motivation. Then the responsibility for the educational or care work is dumped on the person you cannot expect to shoulder it, the service-user. That can be considered quite a cowardly behaviour. If the service-user is to meet certain criteria to receive assistance, we have not only found a way to get rid of our feeling of impotence, we have also made sure of finding an excuse for a defective outcome of the educational work or care. That is the absolutely most effective way to create a foundation to develop inefficient educational and care methods. Therefore it is not only good to take on responsibility in the case in question, it is also an absolute necessity to our work and our development of sound methods.

To dump the responsibility on the service-user by talking about lack of motivation thus gives us several problems:

- We lose the possibility of exerting an influence and consequently also power.

- We increase our feeling of powerlessness and consequently also the risk of being burnt-out.

- We limit our possibilities for developing good methods.

- We cement the negative development of the service-user and may confirm his or her impression that the staff are of no use.

We must therefore regard the feeling that the service-user is unmotivated as a sign that our methods are not good enough and that we therefore must come up with better methods. Swedish psychologist Per Revstedt says that if a client is motivated half the work is done, and that a great part of educational or psychological treatment must therefore be about motivating the person. He goes as far as saying that motivation is always the responsibility of the staff. By shouldering responsibility we can influence and consequently regain the power of our work. To blame the service-user is nothing but a sign of us not managing our work with the methods we are currently using.*

Obstinacy and flexibility

I often hear from parents or staff that a service-user is so stubborn it is difficult to work with him or her. I normally deal with that at once. There are several problems with the concept of obstinacy. First, it is a highly dangerous concept by which to handle a service-user.

> **Angellika** has ADHD. She goes to a special school unit and lives in a foster home. Angellika likes different things. Among other things she likes dresses and music, and she enjoys blowing bubbles through a straw when drinking milk.
>
> One day in the spring of 2006 Angellika is sitting having a snack with the other children in school. She starts to blow in her milk, which makes her teacher tell her to stop. 'I'll stop,' Angellika says, 'in a little while. I'm just going to finish blowing.' Angellika,

---

*   Revstedt 2002.

like many other children with ADHD, has compulsive symptoms, and one of these is that she feels she must blow nine times when she has started to blow.

The teacher reacts strongly to this. He tells her off properly, whereupon Angellika blows a little faster. Then he takes the glass away from her. Angellika is very frustrated over this, and kicks him on the shinbone. He therefore grabs her and puts her down on the floor. She kicks, spits and hits out, so several teachers have to come to help. After about 15 minutes Angellika calms down and starts crying. The teachers let go of her and the situation is over.

This incident does not happen once, but sometimes several times a week. The straw is therefore taken away from Angellika. Then she continues to blow in the milk without a straw. The teachers describe this as obstinacy and are annoyed. They think that Angellika is the one with the power over the situation.

On an ordinary Thursday in May 2006 the situation is repeated. Angellika blows in her milk, the teacher tells her to stop, and she replies: 'I'll stop in a little while. I'm just going to finish blowing.' The teacher takes the glass from her, she kicks, spits and hits out, and the teacher puts her down and holds her until she is calm. However, this time she doesn't begin to cry, but is silent, blue and limp. The teachers call for an ambulance, but Angellika dies in hospital the next day. She was seven years old.

This is a true story. Angellika's second name was Arndt and she died in May 2006. In March 2007 her teacher was convicted of manslaughter and was sentenced to 60 days' imprisonment and the school was charged to pay a fine of $100,000 and was forced to close down.[*]

This kind of restraint is fairly common: the member of staff makes a demand, the service-user refuses, the member of staff sticks to the demand, the service-user tries to get away, the member of staff follows and sticks to the demand, whereupon the service-user beats or kicks. After that the service-user is put down and the incident is

---

[*]   Harter 2007.

described as a reaction to unprovoked violence from the service-user.

Angellika was not a stubborn child who wanted to be in charge, but a girl with great difficulties of inflexibility. That is the second problem with the concept of obstinacy.

Inflexibility is a diagnostic criterion in the autism spectrum and is a commonly described problem of people with ADHD, Tourette's syndrome or intellectual disabilities, and not least of people with Down's syndrome. We can therefore not allow ourselves to use the concept of obstinacy. Inflexibility is often described as one of the prerequisites for our service-users to exist.[*]

Inflexibility is related to compulsive behaviour, which means that we all can relate to it. Everybody has had compulsive behaviour, often in the form of not walking on the lines in the pavement as ten-year-olds. Many of us still have certain compulsive behaviours in stressed situations, for example checking the cooker an extra time when we are on our way out the door.

Inflexibility is a common personal trait that is distributed normally over the population. That means we may all get into situations where our flexibility is tested.

- **Cal** is ten years old. He has no diagnosis and no more problems than other ten-year-olds. He is in other words a completely ordinary boy. Cal loves to play PlayStation. Sometimes when he is sitting in his room playing, his mother enters the room and tells him: 'You must finish now; we're eating now.' Cal normally replies: 'I'll be there in a minute; I'm just going to finish the level.'

- **You** are in a nice restaurant and have ordered fillet of beef with pepper sauce on a bed of vegetables. With the food you are going to have a fine red wine. You cut a piece of meat, put it in your mouth and chew slowly and enjoy. You have a drop of the wine and let it roll over your tongue. The waiter approaches you and says: 'Unfortunately, I have to ask you to leave at once; we must have this table for another customer.' How would that feel and how would you reply? I am certain that you would have

---

[*] Autism: World Health Organization 1992; ADHD: Kadesjö 2001; intellectual disabilities: Wehmeyer 2001.

an unpleasant physical experience and that the prospect of leaving would fill you with anguish.

- For many years I had a grey, long woollen coat that I had been given by my father's superior in 1978. The coat went well with several hats I used, both in style and colour, and I thought I looked quite handsome in it. I used it on and off until the Christmas of 2005 when my partner, Susan, apparently thought it was time for a change. On Christmas Eve I was given a big gift and happily unwrapped it. In it was a winter jacket that had no similarity to my coat. It was made of a leather-like material, was shorter than the coat and much more modern. I was not properly prepared for that gift and was slightly agonized, which apparently showed in my face. Susan said: 'Perhaps you should wait ten minutes before you say anything so you have the time to get used to it.' And quite right, ten minutes later it felt just right and it was obvious that the other coat was worn out and out of date, when I had actually seen what I looked like in the new jacket.

These three situations are about completely ordinary people who do not have problems with flexibility. Still, we can all experience a state of anxiety in situations where our flexibility is challenged. How much greater anxiety might people with difficulties with flexibility have then? Of course many of our service-users will not manage to do as we expect if we make demands on their flexibility. To refuse to go to the table when playing PlayStation is a way to avoid anxiety, and I actually like it when service-users develop strategies to avoid anxiety. That makes my job so much easier. The problem is that staff feel they lose control, but that we have already dealt with.

The third problem with the concept of obstinacy is that when we think the problem is obstinacy we place the responsibility with the service-user. He or she must change if we are going to be able to work. This is, exactly as has been described in the passages on throwing the blame on someone else and on motivation, cowardly. We cannot place responsibility for the educational or care work with the service-user. We must shoulder that ourselves, and there we can be helped by moving the focus from the service-user's will to the service-user's ability. There is then the possibility of exerting an influence by changing demands and needs. Having the responsibility for the educational or care work, we can adjust the work we do so the service-user can overcome their inflexibility. How that is done we will look at in chapter three.

Inflexibility entails much anxiety and sometimes we do not see it. Anxiety may arise because demands are made that the service-users are not prepared for, and then they often simply say no. This no does not mean no in the way we understand it, but more often: 'Give me ten minutes.' If we then prepare the service-user for the demand, it normally works out fine.

Another aspect of inflexibility is the feeling of imbalance. Many people with difficulties with flexibility feel that a situation is not resolved because there is still imbalance.

Joshua is 16 years old. He has always been a lonely boy, but the last few months he has made some friends. They meet up and drink beer that they have bought illegally. Joshua lives with his sister and their parents in a small town where his father is the municipality architect and his mother a doctor at the healthcare centre. The week the following takes place Joshua's father is on a business trip to the US.

One day Joshua is meeting up with his friends at night, but has no money. He therefore goes to the store, grabs a bottle of vodka and runs out the door and away through town. After a couple of hundred metres he begins to walk slowly.

When he is almost home a police car drives up to him. A police officer winds down the window and asks him: 'Joshua, why did you take a bottle of vodka at the store and run?' Joshua does not know how to respond and asks: 'How do you know that was me?' The officer says: 'Everybody knows who you are. If you are going to steal vodka, you'll have to do it in another town.'

Joshua has to go down to the police station to be picked up by his mother. She is angry. She thinks it is embarrassing and awful having to pick him up at the station and tells him off all the way home. When they pass the store Joshua asks: 'Mum, could you buy some vodka for me? My friends are coming over tonight and I promised to get booze.' His mother is terribly angry and says: 'I'll never buy you booze and you won't see your friends tonight. When you steal there are consequences.'

Joshua is calm for a few days. His mother is still angry with him, and he understands that he has to be cautious. After a week he thinks that everything is fine and invites his friends over for the night. He goes downstairs to his mother and asks: 'Mum, may I borrow 20 quid? My friends are coming over tonight and I've promised to get some crisps and soda.' His mother does not believe him and says: 'You intend to buy beer so I won't lend you any money. In fact I won't lend you money for a long time. You stole a bottle of vodka and embarrassed the whole family to the entire town. I won't lend you any money and you won't see your friends tonight!'

Joshua does not think this is fair. He has had his punishment; he was not allowed to see his friends the day he stole the vodka and he has been playing it cool for a whole week. He calls his friends and asks them to bring beer.

At night his friends enter his room through the window so his mother will not discover it. What they have not thought of is that when five 16-year-old boys are sitting smoking hookah and drinking beer in a room on the first floor it is quite obvious when you are sitting on the ground floor watching *Desperate Housewives*. Joshua's mother therefore goes upstairs, barges into his room, throws his friends out and tells him off at the top of her voice. Joshua is also angry; he thinks he has already been punished and that his mother is unfair. Eventually his mother is so angry she boxes his ears.

That has never happened before and Joshua is left speechless. He says goodnight and goes to bed. His mother goes into her room and cries and calls Joshua's father.

In the morning Joshua goes downstairs to the kitchen where his mother is having breakfast. He says: 'I know that I stole a bottle of vodka. Then I wasn't allowed to see my friends. Then I met up with them anyway. Then you hit me. Are we even now?'

'We're not even at all,' his mother says, whereupon Joshua does the only thing he can think of: He gives his mother a box on the ears.

I meet Joshua a couple of days later at a juvenile home and ask him why he is staying there now. He says: 'I'm not totally sure, but I think it's because my parents hit me.'

Joshua still had an imbalance and that entailed an undefined anxiety. He had to remove it. He did his best and it was not exactly what his mother was prepared for.

John is 12 years old and has Asperger's syndrome and ADHD. He goes to special school. One day a boy of nine years takes his cap at the morning break and runs off with it to his friends. They throw it between them for a few minutes until John manages to get hold of it again.

At the lunch break John goes out with a baseball bat in his hands, finds the nine-year-old playing in the sandpit and hits him with full force in the face. When the staff ask him why he did it he says: 'Then he might learn not to take my cap.' And he probably did.

John, just like Joshua, tries to remove an imbalance. By removing the imbalance, the anxiety is minimized. The two boys find it difficult to hold grudges in daily life. If they have a conflict with someone and it is resolved there is no grudge left. The two are also quick to ask for forgiveness, just because it removes imbalances. Some parents and staff find these automatic excuses hard. They think: 'He's not really sorry, he just says he is and then everything should be forgotten. I sure can't forget everything like that.'

If we set out from *People who can behave, will*, that means that in these situations John and Joshua do not manage to behave because that is something they cannot do. This may be to endure the imbalance. Through their behaviours they even out the injustice and move on. In these two cases the people close to them were not inclined to accept their behaviours as a good way of dealing with their anxiety. The two actions were, however, strategies to reduce anxiety.

That is, of course, no excuse, but it places the responsibility for their behaviour with the people close to them, if we want to. We can choose to think that the two boys are badly brought up and perhaps even evil. You hear some people mention psychopathy and a lack of empathy. That is placing the responsibility with the boys, and they probably cannot take it on well enough to create the possibility for good development. If we place the responsibility with ourselves, we have the opportunity to look at how another time we can reduce the anxiety that arises when the boys find themselves in situations they feel are out of balance.

Andrew is 12 years old and goes to a special school. He has a best friend, Will, who he plays with every break. One day something happens at break to make them fall out with each other. They are about to get into a fight when a teacher interrupts them. On their way into the classroom the teacher hears Andrew telling Will: 'It's good we're sitting next to each other. When the teacher looks away I'm going to give you a licking.' The teacher deals with this and says that in this school you cannot fight or threaten anyone. Andrew says: 'That'll be hard because what happened at the break was so damn unfair.'

Andrew therefore has to take his maths book and go to the headmaster's office to do maths. This he thinks is OK. After class the headmaster asks: 'And what are you going to do now?'

'I'm going out to give Will a beating,' Andrew says.

'That you can't do. How about we make a deal? If you don't hit Will at the break, you can have a fudge when you come in again.'

Andrew agrees to that. At break the boys play again without any problems. They are, after all, best friends. After the break Andrew goes to the headmaster and gets his fudge. The headmaster asks: 'And what are you going to do now?' Andrew says: 'I'm going to the classroom to beat Will up.'

Andrew had to spend his classes in the headmaster's office for two days and he had to be bribed with a fudge every break. He stuck to the fact that he was going to beat Will up eventually, but they played well every break.

After two days we had an appointment for guidance and came up with a possible solution. Andrew was summoned to the headmaster who asked him: 'What would it take for you to give up wanting to beat Will?' Andrew had no solution. Then the headmaster proposed a solution that meant that Will would go to the store to buy cream buns. He would have one there. Then

> Andrew would distribute the cream buns to everyone in class,
> but Will. Then they were even. Andrew thought that was a good
> idea. It was carried through and the boys could stay best friends.
> The injustice was settled.

Andrew has great difficulties with flexibility and the unfairness he experienced was getting to him for two days without being reduced. An imbalance can however be reduced in two ways: put more weights on the light side of the scales or remove weight from the heavy side. Andrew's solution was to put something heavy on the light side, the headmaster's to remove something from the heavy side. The balance was however restored and Andrew could move on. This is showing consideration to Andrew's difficulties and adjusting the pedagogy to his needs.

Summary

In order to work in a non-confrontational framework we need to change some of our conceptions about behaviour, both the service-user's and our own. These conceptions often stem from our own childhood, from common misconceptions about behaviour background and from the notion that everybody is equal and that therefore the same demands should be used for everybody.

These misconceptions may be about control: that we can be in control of any situation without the service-user first having self-control in order to trust us. They may be about the cause of challenging behaviour: believing that the service-user manipulates us; or about methods: believing that consistency or punishment is necessary or effective.

Because of the service-user's difficulties with central coherence many of our common methods are ineffective, and we need to use special methods in order to make changes in their lives.

Chapter 3

• • • • • • •

Adjustment of Demands

The easiest explanation of educational and care work is that it is about continuous adjustment of demands and subtle manipulation to achieve the highest possible level of function. However, there are care staff, teachers and psychologists who maintain a view they learnt in their own childhood that educational work and care is about putting the right amount of pressure on somebody to achieve the highest possible level of function. I do not think that these two approaches are necessarily opposites. They may instead be two ways of saying the same thing. Adjusting demands entails applying the correct pressure, or rather the least possible pressure, and allows the service-user to carry out what is demanded. Everybody has the right to say no in any situation. The job of the staff is to make the service users say yes voluntarily.

If a demand is made in a good way and is not too great, the service-user will succeed in carrying through his or her assignment. If the demand is wrong or made in the wrong way, he or she will not succeed. Methods of demand adjustment are crucial if you work with inflexible service-users, and are therefore absolutely necessary in autism, but generally they bring an easier daily life to service-users, parents and staff in other disorders as well.

> **Hassan** is 12 years old and lives at a juvenile home. He is placed there because he has been sexually abused by his mother and therefore should not live at home. He has the diagnosis NLD (nonverbal learning disability).
>
> One of Hassan's tasks is to give water to the horses at the home. When doing so you must first turn off the water in the

enclosed pasture, then go to the cowshed and open the tap, then go back to the pasture and open it there. When the trough is full, you turn off the water in the pasture, then you go to the cowshed and close it, and eventually you return to the pasture to open it so the water in the pipe will not freeze. In other words it is a quite laborious task.

Hassan, as all other 12-year-olds, can be a bit lazy at times. He has discovered that if you start by opening the tap in the cowshed and then run to the enclosed pasture that works fine, and then before the trough is full you run up and turn it off again. In that way you save two rounds between cowshed and pasture.

One day when Hassan has opened the water in the cowshed he sees that the farm cat has had kittens. He sits down to cuddle with them and forgets the time. After 15 minutes he remembers that the water is on and quickly turns it off. He runs down to the pasture and sees that there is water everywhere. He knows that this is a problem; you must remove all waterlogged soil and put gravel around the trough. He starts to walk in circles and makes loud noises as he does when he is anxious and stressed.

Rob, a member of staff, hears him and walks down to him in the pasture. He sees that there is water everywhere and that Hassan is under a lot of stress. He looks away from Hassan and begins to fiddle with the things around the trough and says: 'Will you get a shovel and a wheelbarrow, so we can fix this?' Hassan drifts around for another minute, but after that walks away and returns more collected with a shovel and a wheelbarrow.

Rob solves the situation by making the right demand, and not least by making it in the right way. Hassan knows that he has cheated and partly that his cheating is obvious, and partly that it now will bring a lot of extra work. He cannot handle being confronted with his cheating, and besides Rob thinks that Hassan has already experienced enough unpleasantness in the situation, which is evident from his behaviour. He finds a way for Hassan to divert his attention from what he has done wrong and gives him an outlet from the stress and the situation. He therefore makes a demand that Hassan can live up to without problems.

If Rob had confronted Hassan with what he had done wrong, and then made it clear that Hassan would have to clean up the mess by himself, the situation would probably have ended in conflict. Instead of confronting Hassan and thereby putting him to shame, Rob starts by showing him that they will help one another and concentrate on the task together. He creates a possibility for Hassan to regain self-control. When they are done after half an hour all is restored and Hassan has probably even learnt to handle the water better. In addition, trust in Rob has increased. All in all, a good solution.

Methods of adjusting demands

The demand to go and get a wheelbarrow and a shovel could have been made in many ways. Rob chose the method I call 'demand without pressure'. It is only one of the methods we have at our disposal.

Structure

This is the standard way to adjust demands. However, you must understand what structure is to use it in educational and care contexts, otherwise there is a tendency that the structure is only a way to carry out what the staff or parents wish. Structure is an aid to the service-user to compensate for a lack of *central coherence*, not a way to force the service-user into anything. We should, therefore, never insist on a structure when the service-user cannot deal with it. If compulsion is necessary, we are the ones who have not adjusted the structure enough, not the service-user who is unmotivated, insolent, obstinate or difficult.

Structure creates the possibility to predict. Therefore it is calming and helps to keep self-control.

> **Errol** is 19 years old. He went to a mainstream school until he, at the age of 15, quit going to school. He refused to go and kept to himself at home and played computer games. After a couple of months he was admitted to a youth psychiatric ward and was diagnosed with Asperger's syndrome and social anxiety.

I was contacted because when he was 18 the local authorities wanted to place him in a group home with a school for youths with Asperger's syndrome. The task was to motivate him to move there. One of the reasons was that his mother was moving to a smaller place now that Errol was of age; she lost her accommodation allowance and could no longer afford her former place.

The first thing I did was to change the task. I did not believe it was possible to motivate him, but decided that the public administration and I together would create a structure that ensured his moving. We scheduled preparations for Errol with two talks about where he was going to move, what it looked like where he was going to live and what was the timetable. Then we scheduled a visit to the group home and eventually the move there, where his mother would stay with him for the first week. After that she would go home and start packing for her own move.

We also had a Plan B. If the plan backfired we would just take one step backwards and then forwards again.

All worked according to plan. Errol did not like that he was moving, but accepted it as the reason was that there was no room for him in his mother's new place. He seemingly accepted the plan and carried it through. He visited his new group home and the week when his mother was with him also turned out well.

When his mother went home, he was, however, slightly surprised. When she arrived home, she received a text message from Errol asking her to pick him up at the station. He had taken the train home at the same time as she had left by car. He, who had not left his home for three years, had gone alone to the station, bought a ticket and travelled 400 km by train and arrived at the same time as his mother who had driven.

The public administration called me at once. The official in charge was incredibly stressed with the thought that the whole project had failed. I calmed her down and we took a step backwards and then forwards again. We set a new date a week later, the mother packed up her house and we moved Errol again. He cooperated well and this time he stayed. At his first visit home a few weeks later his mother had moved and it was obvious to him that his home was at the group home. He goes to see his mother one weekend a month and takes the train back and forth by himself.

The structure we used was motivated by the mother's moving, so it made sense to Errol. That is an absolute requirement. People with an intellectual disability do not always have to see a meaning behind the structure. To them it may be enough that there is a structure, whereas logic is often required for a structure to motivate people with a relatively high level of function. To force a structure without motivating a reluctant service-user is on par with abuse and is a violation of individuals' human rights. To use a structure as a help to carry things through that otherwise would have been difficult is on the other hand a good intervention. The structure subdues anxiety and facilitates turns and leaps into the relative uncertainty.

Us-experiences

In his novel *Jenny*, Swedish author Jonas Gardell uses the old pun about two tomatoes crossing a road. Suddenly there is a truck and one of the tomatoes is squashed under the tyre. The other tomato turns around and says: 'Come on ketchup, let's go.'

Gardell uses the pun as an expression of an acceptance of what is different; it does not matter that you have become different, that something has happened to you that has changed you; I want to be with you anyway. Besides, it is you and me, we are an *us*. There is plenty of wisdom in that interpretation. However, I think there is another small truth in the pun. It is much easier to get another person to come along if you go together, 'Come on ketchup, let's go' makes it hard to remain seated.

Visual structure is another way to create such an *us*. It is not about a 'Do you want to come with me?' or 'Now you must go!', but about a motion that is hard to resist. We go together. Visual structure can therefore compensate for the lack of acquiescence we mentioned in chapter one.

Gardell's ketchup effect can also be used in small recurring situations in daily life.

In a school in Malmö, Sweden, they had problems with a class where the children did not want to return to class after the break. The staff most often stood by the classroom and called for a pupil they knew was popular and who would do as they asked. If they made him move towards the classroom the others would follow suit.

This created an us-and-them atmosphere between the class and the teachers and did not contribute to the children coming of their own accord. The teachers were quite frustrated over this.

We introduced another way of working. The teacher went out with the children who usually were playing football, waited 20 seconds and said: 'Come on, let's go inside,' and started walking himself. It turned out that all children followed with no difficulties. Furthermore, it supported the feeling of a 'we' and reduced the teachers' frustration.

When the children feel they are part of a 'we' it is much easier for them to live up to expectations. We move the leadership from the hierarchy of the children to the teacher. This makes it easier for the children to give up some control to the teacher. All in all, a good solution.

Time

This is a fairly common way to adjust how demands are made in special education. It is often used in situations that entail shifts between activities.

Christian is eight years old and has ADHD. He enjoys being outdoors and often plays alone in the garden. His mother has always found it difficult to make him come in when it is time to eat, and making demands has often resulted in conflict.

Finally she comes up with a solution. She calls out the window: 'Christian, five minutes.' A few minutes later she calls that he should come in and eat. Christian comes in without problems. Moreover, the method works in all situations; for example, when he is going to eat, going to bed, going to his grandmother. Christian simply needs to be warned a few minutes before a shift, but he does not need to know what the shift means in advance.

Different service-users are helped by different methods of using time to adjust demands. In the autism field, TimeTimers and other time aids have been used for many years. Egg timers are often used in special school units and in special classes for children with ADHD. However, it is important to find out whether the service-user is able to understand time or needs a clear countdown of the time.

I find time aids very useful myself. When I lecture and do presentations, I have a big digital clock on my computer screen, which I use to estimate how many examples and digressions for each point I am making I have time for. There are however situations where time aids do not work:

> **Daniel,** whom we met previously, and who studies law nowadays, sometimes lectures on his difficulties. However, he finds it incredibly hard to stick to the allotted time. In an attempt to help him with this my colleague gave him a TimeTimer, a small time aid where you set the time you are going to spend, and then can easily follow how much time is left. It is a very visual aid that we have good experiences of. He set it for 45 minutes, which was the time he had at his disposal.
>
> Daniel started to talk, and it worked really well for the first 40 minutes. Then he was clearly nervous, and started talking faster and faster. After a few minutes my colleague had to take away the clock and tell him to take the time he needed.
>
> The problem was that he knew what he wanted to say and was not able to exclude anything. Consequently, he had to talk faster instead.

Similarly it can be difficult to use time aids to make a completely ordinary ten-year-old stop playing PlayStation. Irrespective of when the egg timer rings he will say: 'I'm just going to finish the level.' In the same way you would not manage the previously mentioned situation in the restaurant better, if somebody just when you had tasted the meat and the wine said: 'You've got ten minutes, then we're out of here.' Certain situations have a natural ending and therefore must be allowed to have it. We must therefore add the next method.

Being allowed to finish

I know children who hate mathematics, but cannot deal with turning in a maths problem or a maths page unless they are finished. I myself find it hard to leave a TV movie, even if it is bad, if my partner wants to go to bed. I do want to go to bed as well, but it still takes me a moment to be able to leave the movie. Things that have a natural ending are easiest to leave if you are allowed to finish them.

The advantage of finishing things is that when something is done you say: 'And what are we going to do now?' That makes the shift to the next activity much easier. That is true both for dinner in the restaurant and watching movies, excursions and sleep, but also in many other situations, including when the ten-year-old boy plays PlayStation. If he is allowed to finish the level it is much easier for him to tear himself away from the game than if he has to leave in the middle of it.

Activities with a logical ending are easier to end than situations that are ended actively. We will come back to this shortly when I bring up transition actions. If it is possible to choose an activity with a natural ending, it will make things much easier than if we choose activities that the service-user has to end him- or herself.

Being allowed to finish the different parts of a structured activity is normally safe and good. However, it requires a certain flexibility from those close to the person. That should not be a problem in educational activities or care though, as the staff are there for the service-user, but in a family of several children it may get messy. In that case you ought to create a structure that is so good it is predictable also to the parents, even if you have to wait for the child to finish his or her different activities.

Being allowed to get ready

Hassan, who we met at the beginning of this chapter, has terrible difficulties seeing his mother. Because of the sexual abuse he has suffered from her, he does not live at home and the supervised visits of four hours a month are hard for him. She undresses him and throws his clothes away; she does not want him to wear the clothes he has been given at the juvenile home, but gives him new clothes. The staff do not tell Hassan that he is going to visit his mother in advance, because when he knows it beforehand he is terribly stressed.

One Saturday he is going home for a visit and is awfully stressed when he finds this out. The reason is that he has left his old winter jacket in school and only has his new, good one at the group home. If he puts that one on his mother will throw it away, and he has chosen it himself, it is of a brand that he likes.

Rob, who is driving him, understands that this is difficult. At first they agree upon buying a new jacket if his mother throws it away, but that is not good enough for Hassan. He is very attached to this specific jacket. It is 15 degrees below zero outside, so he must bring the jacket and if he leaves it in the car his mother will make complaints about the juvenile home not making sure he has warm clothes. She often lodges complaints to the municipal executive board, the National Board of Health and Welfare, the county administrative board and anyone else who might listen. Hassan is therefore awfully stressed and anxious already in the morning.

In order to be on time at the mother's, they must leave at noon. Rob who is driving knows this. He also knows that Hassan finds it very hard to get seated in the car when he is under stress and that he needs time in order not to lose self-control. At 11:30 Rob says: 'I'll go out to the car now; come when you are ready to go.'

Hassan begins to walk in circles and make loud noises; his anxiety is obvious. Rob leaves him to collect himself and sits down in the car. Twenty minutes later Hassan has calmed down and goes out to Rob and they can leave.

Rob's behaviour starts out from Hassan having difficulties collecting himself and keeping his self-control.

I talked to a head teacher at a special school in Copenhagen. She said: 'Today we only resort to restraints in one situation. When an excursion is over and we're going back to the school there is always someone who can't handle getting into the bus. It's a situation with a lot of pressure as we must be back at school in time for the end of the school day. So it often ends with us having to grab a pupil and force him onto the bus.'

I do not think that is good enough. By being prepared and flexible, the pupils can, according to my experience, manage to get onto the bus without difficulties. However, a certain professionalism from the teachers is required, as well as an attitude based on the fact that the children do not always succeed, not that they do not want to.

> **Clara** is ten years old. She has autism and moderate intellectual disability. She is in a school for intellectually disabled in a special unit where she is one of six pupils. Clara has considerable difficulties managing change in daily life. If the teacher summons her from the schoolyard to work at her desk, she frequently sits down on the swings and waits until she is ready. This normally takes 45 minutes, even though it is part of a well-known structure.
>
> The teachers have tried to solve this in different ways. She has been forced indoors. This resulted in her being extremely anxious and unable to concentrate on her work. She even hit teachers on a couple of occasions. Alternatively, they have let another pupil sit at her desk. Then she is really anxious and runs into the classroom and pushes the other pupil off and wants to work immediately. She cannot concentrate, however, and learns nothing.
>
> When we put up an extra desk that was only hers and gave her the 45 minutes she needed, she developed well and was calm and secure.

Clara only works for two 30-minute periods a day at her desk, so it does not matter that she gets the time she needs. At home they work in the same way, plenty of planning in advance and enough time to get collected. And Clara has a good life. If we were to force her to follow our schedule we would have had a girl with violently challenging behaviour. Now we have a calm girl who develops well.

> **Lennie** is 22 years old and has autism. He goes to daily life therapy. Lennie often responds forcefully to shifts in activities. The staff may say 'Now you should go to the timetable' and Lennie immediately starts to throw furniture. To the staff this is nothing and they know that it will pass so they let him have his way.
>
> One day a newly employed woman says: 'Lennie, when you're ready we'll go to the timetable.' Lennie remains seated for 15 seconds, then he gets up and walks to the timetable. The staff change to this new way of introducing shifts at once and Lennie stops throwing furniture.

Lennie needs 15 seconds to get ready, but reacts at the word *now*. He has autism and is consequently very concrete in his thinking. He apparently understands the word *now* in a very concrete way, but gets ready for a shift if he feels he gets the time he needs. He needs to feel that he has finished his latest activity, which can be sitting down. He needs very little time to get ready and at the same time keep the feeling of self-control, but cannot handle not being given that time.

Bribes and compensation

We have previously dealt with rewards, and why I call it bribes and compensation. We therefore know that that corresponds to the wages most of us want if we are to go to work. To our service-users, daily life with staff is comparable with working, but few of them get actual pay for being there. There should therefore be room for some bribery or compensation if we are to create a motivation for daily life and for certain particularly difficult demands.

When we use bribes we must make sure that the service-user knows why they are being used and what are the requirements, and that we respect if the service-user does not think that the bribe is big enough. In that case we must let the demand go, like Alex's mother over the visit to the hypermarket in chapter two, or increase the stake. Bribes are there to create motivation and should be considered like wage negotiations in relation to employment. Staff and parents therefore have the same responsibility as staff managers over limiting wage drifts and inflation. We must be able to say no when the bribe or compensation is too great and be satisfied with that.

Sammy is 16 years old and goes to special school in an autism unit. He has autism and is probably of average intelligence, but does not get enough room for his abilities in daily life.

He is good at estimating certain things and likes coke. One day in January he is going to the dentist, and the staff decide that he can do it on his own. He is put on the bus by a teacher and is given money for the fare back to school.

When Sammy is done at the dentist's he goes to a sweet stall nearby and buys coke with the money. He estimates that the coke is worth the walk and chooses to skip the bus. He walks back to school, which takes three hours.

Sammy can estimate and choose. He is developing abilities that will mean a lot to his level of function in the long run. The staff are however stressed when he is not on the bus and have already called the police when he turns up.

On another occasion Sammy suddenly develops a challenging behaviour. He thinks it is great fun to play with the other pupils' timers. You hear the beeping from all rooms, and the other pupils are really stressed when activities suddenly take a much shorter or longer time than normal or when the timer sounds in the middle of an activity that normally does not require a timer.

The staff must therefore come up with a plan. At first they talk to Sammy about it, but he thinks it is fun to horse about with the staff and sees this as a game. It has absolutely no effect. After guidance, the headmaster summons Sammy and says: 'Sammy, we have to make an end to your playing with the timers. I think that we should cut a deal that you let go of playing with them for five days and then you can go to the store with a teacher at school hours and buy a coke. Then there are five new days. When you have bought eight cokes I believe you can let go of them without coke. What do you think about that?'

Sammy thinks that will probably work. They start on the Monday and already on the Friday the first coke is bought with Sammy's own pocket money. Next Friday the second is bought and after eight weeks they stop buying coke, but Sammy does not play with the timers any more.

Sammy could be motivated to stop playing with timers and could also stand that buying coke at school hours ended without starting all over again. He experienced a value in ending the behaviour; a value that was obvious to him and that was worth more than the behaviour itself. It might also be that he understood that this very thing with the timers was important and had to be prioritized.

So far I have described bribes with coke in three case studies. There are of course many different bribes; coke is simply easy and cheap, though not that healthy. You can bribe with activities, solidarity, time for computer games, movie watching, coffee, bus rides, pokemon cards, etc. The simplest and most acceptable bribe for most people is to motivate with story reading or another social activity, but you should not be afraid to use more powerful edible bribes in situations that require a little extra. Those situations are not that many that the service-user will gain weight like wildfire or that the budget is increased uncontrollably. The fear may only be an expression of our tendency towards catastrophe thinking.

Motivating actions

Motivating actions are another way to adjust how we make demands.

Gus is eight years old and has the diagnoses ADHD, Tourette's syndrome and OCD, and has autistic traits as well. He is very clever. Gus likes to swim and loves swimming baths. However, it is really difficult for Gus to leave a swimming pool, as a swimming pool has no natural ending. Gus has no problems handling shifts in activities with a natural ending if he is led into the next activity, but finds it really hard to change activity if he is not allowed to finish in a good way.

Gus's parents and teachers have therefore together tried to find a good way to help him finish the swimming baths. They have tried:

- To set an egg timer for ten minutes and thereby use time. That does not work at all. Gus forgets that the time has been set and is still surprised by the timer when it rings.

- To go to the swimming baths only an hour before closing. The swimming pool attendant then says over the loudspeaker that everybody should get out, which upsets Gus terribly.

- To regulate by saying: 'Now you will swim three times back and forth, and then we're getting out.' This method brings two problems: he begins to swim slowly and starts to play instead and he forgets how many times he has swum back and forth and starts to discuss it.

Then they come up with a good solution: They tell Gus: 'Come on, Gus, let's go to the entrance hall and have a banana.' Gus happily gets out of the pool, showers, gets dressed, and goes to the entrance hall, has his banana and eats it.

A banana has a unique quality: when you have eaten it, it is done and finished. This means that Gus says: 'And what are we doing now?'

This is what I call a motivating action. It is a way of helping Gus manage a difficult shift partly by bribing him a little, partly by creating an ending to an activity he has difficulties ending himself.

Many people with neuropsychiatric problems try themselves to create endings this way by, for example, asking: 'Are we having ice cream before leaving the beach?' By creating a structure that is self-motivating (like ice cream eating) both an ending and possibilities for moving on and handling shifts can be created.

Motivating assistance in shifts

Methods that resemble motivating actions can also be used in other situations.

Isabella is eight years old. She has autism and is violently hyperactive. She goes to a special school group in a larger unit where there also are pupils with physical disabilities.

From the first school day, Isabella is jealous of the children who are in wheelchairs. She thinks that they are cool with their chromed pipes, but also that some of the pupils are pushed around in them. She would want that too.

Isabella finds it incredibly hard to manage shifts. She has great problems getting out of the taxi in the morning, and it is really hard to get her into the taxi in the afternoon. The staff bring up the situation in guidance and we create a transition action.

They buy a wheelchair for Isabella. It is only used for transport to and from the taxi. Isabella is overjoyed. She is pushed to the taxi and when the wheelchair is hoisted into the taxi she sits down in her seat. She happily gets out of the taxi to sit in the wheelchair in the morning and happily leaves it when she arrives at her desk. The wheelchair is for transport, not sitting, which she knows, and it is no problem.

Here the transition action is a clear motivator, almost like a bribe, but is still defined by the situation. Isabella succeeds with the difficult shift and a good structure for the beginning and ending of the school day is created.

Benjamin is 11 years old and goes to special school. He finds shifts really difficult. His greatest problem is also getting out of the taxi and into the school. His teacher, Liza, is a clever person and comes up with a good solution one day. She sits down in the taxi next to Benjamin and says: 'I'm Spiderman.' Then she turns her right hand into the same shape as Spiderman does when he shoots spider-webs and says: 'Fsiuuuww' in the direction of the school. 'I hit the main door. Now it's your turn.' She runs to the door. Benjamin runs after, shoots spider-webs and says: 'I hit inside the corridor.' This way they get into the classroom.

In this case the transition action becomes a diversion. Benjamin can go under his own steam and gets something to think of other than staying in the taxi.

Demands without pressure

Linus is 23 years old. He attends daily life therapy and does not like his job. Linus, like many other people with mental disabilities, suffers from insomnia; he has difficulties falling asleep at night, he sleeps restlessly and wakes up often and finds getting out of bed in the morning difficult.

The staff at his group home have terrible difficulties getting Linus to his daily life therapy. They wake him up by eight in the morning, which rarely has an effect. Then they go to him after ten minutes and wake him up again. After another 15 minutes they usually grab him, which sometimes ends in screaming and conflict. The staff say that if he has not got up at the first two calls he will not get up and go to daily life therapy at all. Linus has an absence of 75 per cent.

After guidance the staff try another strategy. They start waking Linus at 7:30 with the words: 'It's seven thirty, you're going to work at nine.' Then they wait 15 minutes and wake him again with the words: 'It's a quarter to eight, you're going to work at nine.' They use the same intonation as the first time. At eight they repeat the procedure again, the same intonation, the same message and no additional pressure. If Linus does not get up before nine o'clock they stop trying to wake him and let him sleep.

The results were discouraging the first two days. Linus slept all morning. The third day he got up at ten minutes past eight and subsequently he often got up in time to go to work. By reducing the pressure on Linus, his attendance at daily life therapy increased from 25 to 75 per cent.

By removing the pressure from the situation, the staff created the possibility for Linus to take control of himself. When they tried with increasing pressure he did not manage to get out of bed, because the increased pressure meant reduced possibilities for Linus to keep his self-control.

Another standard situation is when a teacher tries to make a pupil get the maths book out, and no matter how much you remind him or her nothing happens. You can then stand by the pupil's desk and say: 'I'll stand here until you get it out.' That is rarely a good strategy. The pupil finds it hard to act and is unnecessarily stressed. If another teacher comes into the classroom instead and says: 'Haven't you got your maths book out yet?', it normally works. The pressure is personal, the reminder is not.

Choices

Having a choice can open up a way out of a situation. People with low acquiescence are particularly helped by getting options. They simply do not have to subordinate themselves; at the same time the staff or parents still structure the situation.

Many people with intellectual disabilities are, however, not able to manage too many options, and the question 'What do you want to do now?' can be far too big. It is, however, possible to reduce the options at the same time as they are made clear.

Options do not have to mean a loose structure either. There being a choice can be a part of a structure, and a limited number of options may further structure the situation. The reader might remember the story about Endra who got to choose between two sets of clothes in chapter one. By bringing her two sets of clothes, Endra's parents structured the choice of clothes without challenging Endra's low acquiescence. At the same time it was easy for Endra to pick clothes that were suited for weather and season.

All these methods of adjusting how we make demands have the same aim: to make sure that the service-user has the optimal resources to keep self-control. Accordingly, he or she will find it much easier to leave control to us, and we all get a much easier time making daily life work.

Ability to respond to demands

We must carefully consider the demands we make. Is it a demand the service-user normally lives up to? Is he or she able to keep partial demands apart? Is he or she able to do it right now?

When I started school in 1972 my teacher could have said: 'Welcome to school. Here we'll learn to read, write and count. Here you have a good book by George Orwell. It's called *1984*. Go home and come back on 6 September 1980 and then we'll discuss it.'

She did not do so. She started by teaching us the alphabet. Then she taught us to piece the letters together to form words, and then to understand and relate to text. And so by 6 September 1980 we could discuss the book *1984* by George Orwell. She did not make one single demand, but countless smaller demands in these eight years, but we made it. You could say that instead of making all the demands at once she made them one at a time.

That is a good principle in adjustment of demands:

Do not make too many demands at once.

Some people can deal with several demands at the same time. We can tell some children to go out to the garden to play, and they put on outdoor clothes of their own accord. Other children need to be told each demand separately: put on your jacket. Put on your boots. Wear the trouser legs outside your boots. Now you can run outside.

In the autism field, this has been polished to perfection. For 30 years Division TEACCH in the US have worked with creating structured learning and skill development techniques for people with autism, and their methods can be used by many more people than those who work with autism. Pictograms, work systems, structures and lists can help many people through daily life. What we have to do is to make sure that we do not make too many demands at once, but divide them into several smaller demands that are adjusted to every service-user's specific ability to respond.

Some days we can all do more than on other days. The same is true for service-users, whose ability to respond may vary considerably according to affective state or mood. In fact, people with an intellectual disability or neuropsychiatric disorder are more likely than people in the general population to be adversely affected by low mood for two reasons. First, their condition may often give them an additional reason to be in a low mood; and second, their condition often denies them the mechanisms to deal with it. Staff and parents should therefore always try to be sensitive to the changing moods of those in their care, taking this into account and adjusting demands accordingly.

A teacher once asked me in a guidance session: 'How come that my four pupils with autism all know how to tie their shoes after an English class, but after gym class they all of a sudden do not? Then they sit down whining and ask me to do it for them. I know that they are able to so I refuse. Then they remain seated until the end of the break and then they usually are able to do it. Is it because they want to manipulate me into fastening their shoelaces?'

One of the oddest sports in the Winter Olympics is biathlon. First you have to ski really fast and then shoot at a target with a rifle. The sport makes great demands on a skill that few other sports do: the ability to keep your levels of adrenaline down. If I were to ski really fast I would not dare even to touch a rifle afterwards. There would be an immediate danger of accidental shots and no precision whatsoever. I would have far too much adrenaline in my blood.

The pupils with the laced shoes would probably not make good biathletes either. After gym class they cannot even tie their shoes. They lose skills they otherwise have because the levels of adrenaline have been too high when they have been running and had exercise. That happens to all of us, except possibly skilled biathletes. None of us are able to do things we find hard when we are under pressure. Then we stick to what we really know.

This means that we must make demands adjusted to what we can expect the service-user to be able to do the moment the demand is made. Some pupils know division on Tuesdays, but not on Mondays. I can keep my papers in order when I do not have too much on my plate, but if I am too busy my orderliness is poor. Some people know how to wash their hair when they are feeling well, but not when they are feeling unwell.

If we are of the opinion that everybody who can behave will, we naturally must make our demands within the limits of the service-user's abilities.

Summary

Everybody has the right to say no. If we are to work in an atmosphere of peace, we need to take on the responsibility of the demands we put on the service-users. If we get a no we probably did not make the demand in the right way. The ways we get a yes are by making it easy for the service-user to say yes, using methods as structure, us-experiences, choice, letting people finish or get ready, or simply by changing the demand. By taking on the responsibility of the yes we keep the possibility of changing the situation, whereas by placing the responsibility of the yes on the service-user we let go of power.

Chapter 4

• • • • • • •

Stress Factors: A Model
for Explaining Chaos

This is the most theoretical chapter. It is also an important chapter. The rest of the book is about how we manage behavioural problems in the short term, while this chapter is about how we prevent behavioural problems and work with them in the long term. We will deal with possible reasons for different behaviours, but also how these can be removed. All so you as a parent or member of staff will be able to take responsibility and bring positive changes into the service-user's life.

The effects of stress

Stress has often been described as the reason for irrational behaviour in people. Stress research originates from research on soldiers partaking in the First World War, both on the symptoms some of them developed from the strain in the trenches and on the reasons for certain pilots crashing with their planes outside the war zone. They were interested in reasons for irrational behaviour.

A researcher and theorist who has focused on stress in earnest is Richard S. Lazarus. He described stress as a causal factor in different kinds of behaviour, not least in the development of different diseases. Partly he described stress, partly different ways of dealing with stress, which he named *coping*. Lazarus is of the opinion that certain people can endure stress because they have good strategies for mastering difficulties they encounter in daily life. Coping is consequently the strategies people have for managing stress. If you have good coping strategies you are able to manage stress better than if you have poor coping strategies.[*]

Lazarus' research focuses on the factors that make us develop different difficulties in life, among other things anxiety, depression and psychosis. His idea is that different stresses combine in the development of difficulties.

Stress research has not been particularly interesting to theorists and clinicians that have worked with neuropsychiatric disorders. The background to this is that Bruno Bettelheim in the 1950s introduced the concept 'refrigerator mother'. It was an explanatory model of the development of autism, where attachment and the mother's possible impact were given plenty of prominence. Today we know that the most important factors in the development of autism and ADHD are genetic, but there still are voices that claim differently. For example, in the last few years we have heard very much about environmental toxins, vaccinations, sugar or poor upbringing as explanatory models of neuropsychiatric disorders or of the behavioural problems children with these disorders may have. These explanatory models have however not proven valid.

Psychologists and researchers who work with neuropsychiatric disorders have consequently not wished to bring stress into the debate that much. There is always a risk that some people begin to talk about stress as a causal factor for the symptoms that define disorders in the neuropsychiatric field; something no one wants.

Therefore the attempts to talk about stress have focused on stress as the result of neuropsychiatric disorders. For example, Tony Attwood has written about stress caused by difficulties with social interplay, communication and flexibility as well as describing the stress that difficulties with perception bring (for example sensitivity of sound). In that way, the concept of autism is saved from being the result of stress.

In the same way, coping has been described in other terms than is done with people without autism. Attwood has described coping in the form of:

---

[*]   Lazarus 1999.

- special interests – where you manage the stress you are exposed to better if you specifically focus on what you are interested in

- compensating cognitive understanding – meaning that people with autism must figure out why other people do as they do contrary to people without autism who are able to put themselves in another person's shoes and consequently understand this intuitively

- activities – for example running, playing tennis, doing breathing exercises or playing a relaxing CD.

Most of these set out from educational interventions. Attwood's focus on coping is how to help people with autism manage their stress, not on how the person's own strategies of managing his or her world are.[*] Consequently, there is hardly any connection between general stress research and the autism stress research.

In the last few years there has been some research on stress and coping in people with intellectual disabilities. Among other things, several researchers have found a connection between life events and challenging behaviour or depression in people with mental retardation. It has been shown that life events cause challenging behaviour regardless of being negative (such as the loss of a parent) or positive (such as entering a romantic relationship).

In the 1970s, stress was already being looked at as a contributing factor in the development and maintenance of symptoms of psychosis in people with schizophrenia. Nuechterlein and Dawson outlined what is called the diathesis-stress model in 1984.[**] They described psychosis as the result of too high stress levels over time and described treatment directed at stress factors as a powerful treatment of symptoms in schizophrenia (Figure 4.1).

They depict a development over time where the stress keeps increasing until eventually a certain level is reached and psychotic symptoms are released. Before such levels are reached there are certain warning signs, for example problems managing one's hygiene. In

---

[*]   Attwood 2006.

[**]   Nuechterlein and Dawson 1984.

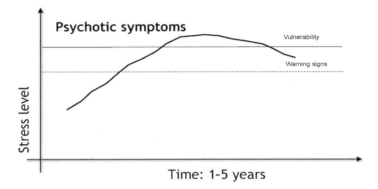

**Figure 4.1 Psychosis as the result of too high stress levels over time –
Nuechterlein and Dawson's diathesis-stress model**

active treatment, the symptoms disappear first, and in time also the warning signs.

A colleague, Trine Uhrskov, and I have developed this model further so it can be used as a frame of understanding for behavioural problems and other secondary problems in neuropsychiatric disorders, intellectual disabilities and brain damage. Therefore in this chapter I often use *we* instead of *I* to refer to our common work.

We cannot explain the basic symptoms in neuropsychiatric disorders by stress. We can however explain challenging behaviour and the depressive or anxiety-filled periods many people with these diagnoses have, and we can create an understanding for some of the problems you as a parent or member of staff experience over service-users' behaviour.*

Whereas Nuechterlein and Dawson's diathesis-stress model is based on development over several years, we have concentrated on short periods of time, for example one day or an hour. Then we do not talk about symptoms of psychosis but of chaos: if the stress is too high in a short perspective, the service-user loses self-control and

---

*   Uhrskov and Hejlskov Jørgensen 2007.

experiences chaos. The chaos can take the form of violent anxiety attacks, violent, extrovert behaviour or violent self-harm.

We would want an ordinary day in our service-users' life to be as shown in Figure 4.2.

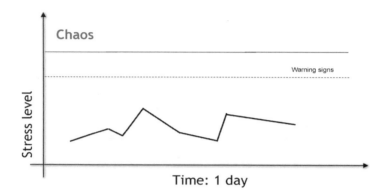

Figure 4.2 An ideal day in a service-user's life

However, our service-users' days more often look like Figure 4.3.

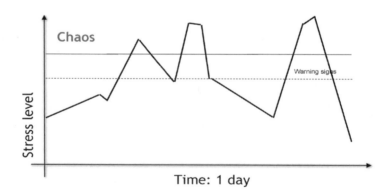

Figure 4.3 A typical day for some service users

Some of our service-users have days when they do not reach the level of warning signs and others rarely have such days. If we are able as staff or parents to adjust daily life to accommodate our service-users, we can perhaps keep the chaos at bay, but the warning signs we will probably have to live with. That we do in our own lives as well. For example, some people get compulsive symptoms when they are going on holiday and must check all windows and doors an extra time, something that is not necessary if they are just going to work. In the same way we ask our children to stay quiet when we are driving onboard a ferry. We cannot manage noise and talking when we do something that demands a little extra from us.

Some researchers have described the ability to stand stress as being much lower in people with neuropsychiatric disorders compared to other people.[*] This may be true, but you can also look at it from another point of view. It may be that there are more stressful factors in our service-users' lives.

Some of the stresses and stress factors that make it hard to take care of oneself are basic and fundamental. Aaron Antonovsky describes some chronic risk factors for faulty development that are reminiscent of these. However, he focuses a lot on factors in the family, whereas we focus more on factors that interact with the difficulties people with neuropsychiatric disorders or intellectual disabilities have.[**]

That a stress factor is basic means that it is present in the service-user's life every day and that the space between the basic stress and the chaos limit is much smaller than in other people. An example of one of these is sleep disorders. We have all slept badly sometimes and felt how hard it is to carry out what you normally would be able to the following day. This may be represented as in Figure 4.4.

The space up to the chaos experience or the warning signs is much smaller than normal. To have slept poorly is a stress factor that is ongoing all day; it becomes basic. Sleep disorders in neuropsychiatric disorders are considered a common symptom. Many other basic stress factors are combinations of symptoms and environmental factors. If you have poor central coherence, it only becomes a problem if the

---

[*]   Groden, Baron and Groden 2006.

[**]   Antonovsky 1991.

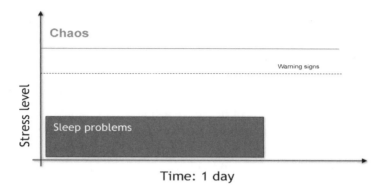

Figure 4.4 The effect of sleep problems on a day's baseline stress level

structure in your everyday life is not sufficient. Likewise, if you have sensory difficulties concerning vision and sound, it is only a problem if your surroundings are loud and messy.

If you have several such stress factors in your life, it is hard to manage (as shown in Figure 4.5).

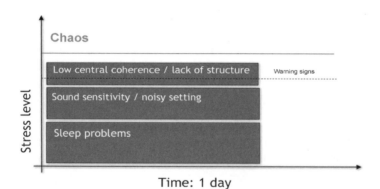

Figure 4.5 The effect of multiple stress factors on a day's baseline stress levels

The example in Figure 4.5 is taken from a boy we have worked with. We identified these three basic stress factors of his. Probably there are many more, but this was enough for an illustration and a treatment plan. He describes how hard it is for him to fall asleep at night, how hard it is to wake up in the morning and how tired he often is in the day. Furthermore, he describes that he has great difficulties understanding causes and effects in daily life and how he must concentrate all the time. Still he is surprised by the consequences of his actions, and is also anxious when he comes to think of what might happen in a moment or two. Moreover, he finds it hard to manage noise and reacts strongly to being outdoors, going by bus or the tube, and also reacts to other service-users' noise. If these three stress factors take up most of his capacity, this means that he has real difficulties managing an ordinary day. If we put the ideal curve of daily life on top of his basic stress factors we get the pattern depicted in Figure 4.6.

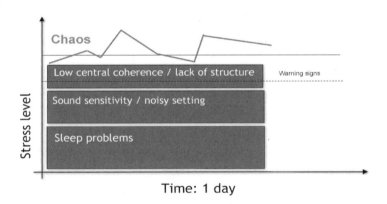

Figure 4.6 The effect of multiple stress factors on the curve of an ideal day

He experiences chaos several times a day, despite fairly mild brief stress.

These brief stresses can also be described as situational or passing. They may be demand situations or setbacks or they may be something that you have not predicted. This is what happens when you are going on holiday and it is hard to be off, or what happens when somebody tells us we must return the plate with a just-started fillet of beef.

Situational stress factors lie on top of the basic factors and are consequently very obvious to the people around the service-user (Figure 4.7). We see them as triggering factors of chaos and therefore try to avoid them.

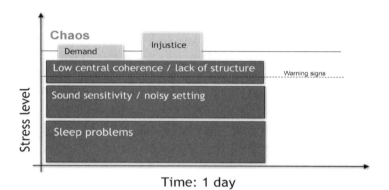

Figure 4.7 The effect of adding situational stress factors to basic stress factors

Staff and parents often focus the care and educational work around the situational stress factors. We pave the way and remove obstacles, and in that way limit the service-users' lives so they will not be stressed. The problem with this kind of care is that we must run very fast to have the time to save our service-users from all stressful experiences. It may be much easier to remove some basic stress factors. Then we do not have to run as fast and the service-user gets a more stable life.

Another aspect of this is that some of the situational stress factors are the experiences that give us something out of the ordinary. I see my life as a daily life of work, dinner, sleep, breakfast, etc., but if this was all that constituted my life it would be pretty boring. I bring life meaning through experiences: a weekend in a small hotel by the sea with good food and walks on the beach, a trip to Italy in my holidays, Christmas with all the children, my favourite radio show on Saturdays, and so on. These experiences are not stress-free, and even though they bring my life meaning and energy they also bring impressions and consequently stress. Lazarus has described getting married as one of the big life events that brings the most stress, despite it being a happy occasion.

If we work mostly in the situational field there will be no trips to the sea. The quality of life will decrease, but daily life may be better. If we mostly work with the basic stress factors, the service-user will manage the situational stress factors and thereby have a higher quality of life without a mental overload as the result.

Basic stress factors

There are many examples of stress factors. I have collected my own in my clinical work, but also by introducing the model and asking people with different difficulties which factors take up room in their lives. Some of them are reminiscent of Tony Attwood's descriptions of stress whereas others have a completely different point of departure. You must however keep in mind that these are only examples. The service-users you meet in daily life may have many more.

The basic stress factors I have encountered most often, and which I discuss more fully below, are:

- poor central coherence
- executive difficulties
- lack of structure
- sleep disorders
- sensory mental overload
- daily life characterized by too high or too many demands
- family-related problems
- teenage existence
- loneliness
- alienation
- strong emotions in people close by
- December
- great life events
- pollen allergy

- pain conditions
- relationship problems.

Poor central coherence

If you have difficulties understanding causes and effects, it is really hard to predict not only other people's behaviour, but also what might happen. Life therefore is often insecure and characterized by anxiety, and there is a lot of insecurity in daily life. This often brings different symptoms.

When you increase the structure around the service-user, the consequences of a poor central coherence are often reduced and the stress factor minimized. This is due to the fact that the service-user does not have to worry about what might happen, but gets a greater predictability in daily life. The autism method TEACCH is based on this understanding.

Executive difficulties

These can affect the ability to plan and carry out things or the ability to hold back impulses, and in relation to a poor central coherence the ability to understand the consequences of one's actions.

We know that people with brain damage in the frontal parts of the brain develop severe executive difficulties, and we also know that they are incredibly sensitive to stress and need clear frames, structure and a calm daily life to function reasonably.

Lack of structure

This is a common experience that has to do with the problems concerning lack of central coherence, but as experienced by the service-users themselves. By making sure that the structure is correctly adjusted we can compensate for some executive difficulties and for poor central coherence.

Sleep disorders

Sleep disorders are more common than we think. Remarkably, many people with neuropsychiatric disorders have great difficulties over sleep. For example, it has been shown that over 30 per cent of

8- to 12-year-olds and at least 75 per cent of adults with Asperger's syndrome have severe sleep disorders and that more than 70 per cent of children with ADHD have sleep disorders.[*]

In our self-understanding groups (I have for a few years developed and carried out a concept of self-understanding groups for youths with Asperger's syndrome with psychologist Trine Uhrskov) far more than half of the youths have problems sleeping that were far beyond common sleep disorders in youth.

In the last few years this has begun to be taken more seriously and today there are effective medicines with the sleep hormone melatonin that may facilitate life for many of our service-users.

Sensory mental overload

Many people with neuropsychiatric disorders have great difficulties sorting their impressions. A small baby has the same problems, but solves it by screaming or falling asleep if he or she is over-stimulated. Our service-users sometimes solve it by hitting the staff, screaming or biting their hands. These are chaos signs or warning signs. This sensory mental overload based on sensory difficulties may be caused by:

- noise or unpredictable sounds
- messy surroundings
- touch and pressure sense difficulties
- pain.

NOISE OR UNPREDICTABLE SOUNDS

Hanna is 57 years old and has a so-called right hemisphere disorder. She appears fairly autistic and lives in an institution for elderly intellectually impaired people. Hanna is very active and outgoing, and has difficulties calming down. She reacts to all small noises and uses a great part of her day to scold the other

---

[*]   Allik, Larsson and Smedje 2006; Paavonen *et al.* 2003; Sung *et al.* 2008; Tani *et al.* 2003; Turk 2003; van der Heijden *et al.* 2007

residents because they make noises, for example smacking their lips or talking to themselves.

Hanna is only calm when she is lying in her bed at night or when she listens to her favourite group, The Cult, really loudly. The staff have arranged a music room for her where she can play as loud as she wants. She says: 'When the music is really loud you can't hear anything else.' The good thing about just listening to The Cult is the even sound pressure; that is why she likes them.

Hanna like so many others with neuropsychiatric disorders reacts to small sounds. The sounds we screen and filter out she finds hard to keep out. She hears the ventilation, small children walking by in the street and other people talking to themselves and feels like they are directed at her. This means that she all the time must think of sounds and consciously filter them out. Of course she does not have much surplus in daily life; she is constantly overworking.

MESSY SURROUNDINGS

Some people find visual impressions very stressful. These may be the number of colours in a room or the number of things. You can easily imagine this for yourself: if you enter a room that is white through and through, where the ceiling is high and the proportions are good, this feels calmer than entering a small room of many colours.

TOUCH AND PRESSURE SENSE DIFFICULTIES

Some of our service-users have a very different tactile sense where the pain threshold may be heightened or very low, where the experience of temperature is different, where you find light touch difficult and prefer harder pressure.

Some treatments that set out from this kind of difficulty have been developed, for example brushing, tactile stimulation, ball blankets, wrist weights, deep pressure clothing (broad belts under the clothes, compression stockings, etc.) and transcutaneous electrical nerve stimulation (TENS) (low-level electrical stimulation of muscles).

Jessica, who we met in chapter one, is 21 years old today. She has autism, and ever since she was a small child she has hurt herself when upset. She started biting her hand and later developed this to slapping her face when she was about ten years old.

Her parents and staff in school reacted strongly to this. She was in a school where there also were some children with cerebral palsy, so they took an aid meant for these children – an arm stretcher – and used it for Jessica. This meant that she could not hit herself in the face or bite her hand.

When I entered the case she had been fastened in a bed with arm stretcher attached for several years. She told me that she was afraid of her arms. The staff described her as incredibly sensitive to stress. My task was to make her get out of the fastening and the arm stretchers, as these were illegal aids.

We started by introducing a ball blanket ten minutes a day after her bath, and she was not allowed to wear her arm stretchers in that short while. Then the period of time was successively increased until she could ask for the ball blanket herself. Then we introduced a kidney belt, rather like motorbikers wear, to keep an even pressure around her waist, under her clothes. We also introduced compression stockings for the same reason.

At the same time all unnecessary things were taken out of her room to give it a tidier impression.

After only a few weeks she herself asked to have the aluminium bars removed from her arm stretchers thereby making them soft and bendable, and after a couple of months she could manage daily life without being fastened in bed. She still hit herself sometimes when she was stressed or scratched herself making a small wound on her hand for a while, but none of this behaviour was considered dangerous.

Some of our service-users experience this kind of stress factor for a shorter period of time, for example when they get new clothes or when they are changing from summer to winter clothes or the other way round. It can be unbelievably hard to make some people stop wearing a hat in spring![*]

---

[*]   Fisher *et al.* 1998; Hanley *et al.* 1998. .

PAIN

Pain is a sensory input that has recently surfaced as a factor in self-harm. We use pain killers to reduce self-harm, and our experience is that it reduces self-harm up to 50 per cent. The theory is that self-harm is often used to manage self-control in the short run, as previously described, but that the pain unfortunately does not fade fast enough. After a short while the pain becomes a basic stress factor and thereby induces further self-harm. The pain you inflict on yourself means that the behaviour remains, making a vicious circle. By steadily administering pain killers the pain as a stress factor can be removed, and self-harm reduced markedly.

Daily life characterized by too high or too many demands

These may be your own demands on yourself or other people's demands.

Your own demands may include demands on success, demands to be ordinary, to behave correctly, to manage to do all your homework, etc. This is mostly a problem for service-users who manage quite well and therefore consider themselves fairly ordinary. Furthermore, some people with autism symptoms have difficulties comparing themselves to other people and work very hard to make sure that other people do not discover that they are different, even though it is obvious to most people.

> **Sean** is 22 years old and has Asperger's syndrome. He spends a lot of energy trying to figure out how to appear normal. When people say hello to him he never answers. He does not know how to say hello in a good way and he does not want to appear strange. He thinks he appears more normal when he does not answer.

Other people's demands include, for example, demands from parents to do well in school, or demands from work or school. The problem is not the demands themselves (they are situational stress factors) but the feeling of living a life filled with demands. This can be compared to the stress most people experience at times and that sometimes leads to burnouts and depression.

Family-related problems

These may be:

- conflicts with parents about daily life or what you are able to do yourself, even as an adult with mental retardation or neuropsychiatric problems

- conflicts with siblings, for example about hierarchy if the service-user is the oldest

- conflicts between parents or between other family members

- social problems in the family, for example alcoholism, lack of structure, violence.

We think that it is important to put family-related problems as one of many stress factors instead of seeing them as the critical factor of a person's level of function, which often is the case in the ADHD field and in psychodynamic contexts. However, we do think that it is important to see family-related problems as part of the total number of problems, and not ignore them because a psychiatrist has made a diagnosis, which has often happened in the autism field.

Teenage existence

When we were teenagers ourselves we experienced for a few years some of the warning signs that are often blamed on hormones. These may be emotional lability, sleep disorders, irritability, etc. In the diathesis-stress model (see Figure 4.1), the stress of forming one's own identity and taking stands on the great existential questions about what you want to do with your life, what is the meaning of life, etc. that most young people are faced with, is specified as one of the causes of psychosis often developed in youth. In my opinion, the existential questions are stress factors that for a few years take up a lot of room in a person's young life. Besides, the period between childhood and established adulthood we call youth is often longer if you have ADHD or Asperger's syndrome, which means that these stress factors can be present up to ten years.[*]

---

[*]   Tantam 2003.

Loneliness

Many people with neuropsychiatric problems feel lonely for long periods of time. In the autism spectrum this is often the consequence of difficulties taking part in social interplay and consequently making friends, whereas in ADHD it may be the result of friends finding it hard to manage impulsivity or unreliability over keeping agreements, etc.

I have found that if you create a forum where people with neuropsychiatric problems can meet, this often has a great effect on their wellbeing. My colleague Hanne Veje has for a couple of years had a social club for young people with Asperger's syndrome or nonverbal learning disorder, and has noticed that even if the rest of the life does not work, the club night every second week is prioritized. Many people describe that for the first time in their life they have felt involved in social contexts. The meeting places for people with neuropsychiatric problems who go to mainstream schools or to ordinary jobs are very few because they often have difficulties creating relationships with people without these kinds of problems. So it may be easier for people with a greater need of assistance to meet friends in care contexts.

Alienation

Alienation is another aspect of loneliness experienced by many people. When you feel different from other people, that often involves stress, especially in your youth. This can unfortunately not be compensated for with a club for the like-minded, but may even be a painful feeling that is yet more painful when among people with similar difficulties.

Strong emotions in people close by

There is a vast amount of research that describes how so called expressed emotion, strong emotions expressed openly, particularly negative ones like anger and irritation, towards patients with schizophrenia are a significant factor in whether they will manage without relapse in psychosis. In the diathesis-stress model (see Figure 4.1) this means that strong emotions are an important stress factor.

They have also proved to be a significant factor for the course of events in bipolar disorder, alcoholism and for the wellbeing of children with intellectual disabilities. Furthermore, in the last few years several researchers have shown connections between strong emotions in people close by and challenging behaviour in children and adults with mental retardation and in young people and adults with autism.[*]

In our model, we consider the strong emotions a stress factor among many others, but an important one. We will later on see how this can be, but regarding the stress model it is important to know that if we can minimize our irritability, stop being angry, be moderately happy instead of overjoyed and avoid stressing and pushing the service-user by stressing ourselves, the service-user will manage his or her daily life better. We should be a little more relaxed in our ways.

December

In the month of December (or through Ramadan) a lot more happens than in an ordinary month. Expectations for Christmas over gifts and how nice and cosy it will be take up a lot of room, as does the fact that daily life is interrupted by Christmas preparations, both in school and in therapy. We decorate and clean and we are all slightly different in our ways. This is felt as a big stress factor both for service-users and staff and means that December is a time of more incidents than usual in different activities. Often both staff and service-users (and some parents) breathe a sigh of relief at the beginning of January.

Great life events

These may include losing a parent, moving, changing jobs, school or daily life therapy. There is a great amount of research that shows that these great events entail stress levels that may take quite a long time to bring down. In 1967, Holmes and Rahes described various events and specified how hard they were to adjust to. Their list

---

[*]   Greenberg, Seltzer and Hong 2006; Hastings *et al.* 2006; Lam, Giles and
        Lavander 2003; O'Farrell *et al.* 1998; Simoneau *et al.* 1998; Weigel *et al.* 2006.

contains events like the death of a spouse, divorce, illness, getting married, having a baby and great personal success. They believe that the greater the number of big life events you are subjected to for a period of a couple of years, the greater is the risk of falling ill in both somatic and psychiatric diseases. In our terminology we could say that a life event may result in a basic stress factor for quite a long time.*

In neuropsychiatric disorders or in intellectual disabilities these life events may be even bigger experiences for the person in question. To move can be incredibly hard. Losing a parent, who has taken on a much greater responsibility than is otherwise done, can be very difficult, not only because you miss the person, but because it affects so many other things in life.

Most people with special needs live in a fairly small world, which means that a small change is really big for them in relation to the size of their life and world. Most people manage to move because the greatest part of their lives will not change only because their house does, but if you spend most of your time at home this is an altogether different matter.

Pollen allergy

In the same way that December is a stressful month, the pollen season is a basic stress factor for a period of time every year. I get many more emergency calls from staff in the pollen season than in any other month of the year. Therefore I normally ask if the service-user is medicated to pollen allergy if I get an inquiry for guidance from April to June. Often challenging behaviour can be removed simply by keeping the allergic symptoms down.

---

*   Examples of research that have shown how great life events also are an important factor for people with intellectual disabilities or neuropsychiatric disorders are: Esbensen and Benson (2006), who found connections between great life events and challenging behaviour in people with intellectual disabilities; Tsakanikos *et al.* (2007), who showed that you can do a risk assessment of challenging behaviour from life events.

Pain conditions

People with different pain conditions have more challenging behaviour when in pain. Pain conditions are not uncommon in people with intellectual disabilities. These may be connected to physical disabilities or joint problems related to hereditary syndromes. In service-users with no language, their behaviour may be the only indicator of the level of pain, and in others it may be very difficult for the service-user to connect the pain with how he or she is feeling generally.

Lizette is 17 years old and has autism and intellectial disabilities. She started hurting herself at an early age, among other things by hitting her ulnar nerve and by biting her hand. She has no language. To make sure she would not hurt herself, her family started to tie her up in bed when she was not in school, and tie a strap around her body and arms under her outdoor clothes when they were outdoors.

When Lizette grew, doctors discovered she did not grow evenly. Her legs were not developing evenly and she was hipped. She was operated on a couple of times, but she could not be completely cured. Her condition was considered to be connected with some pain.

When she was 13, she started to hurt herself more and her parents began to hold her arms behind her back when she was not protected by straps or fastening. In school they embraced this and began to fasten her arms when she wanted to hurt herself.

At the age of 17 Lizette is a costly girl. She needs three people around her at all times as her arms are held so she will not hurt herself. It is very physically demanding to hold her. Lizette does not want to sit down but stands up all day. She reacts strongly to who is holding her and scratches and kicks staff she dislikes.

Lizette's parents are against medication. They have denied Lizette having so-called antipsychotics that are often effective with self-injurious behaviour, and do not think that she should have any stronger medication than aspirin. After talking to doctors however they agreed to try a stronger pain medication and immediately an improvement was visible in Lizette. She was suddenly not as sensitive to who was working with her and was happy for many hours every day. She stopped scratching and kicking and could sit down.

Unfortunately, her parents stopped giving her the medication because they feel they cannot read her when she is given pain medication, and consequently are not able to adjust her day accordingly. The staff in school and at the short-time care where she spends some weekends think this is really hard, but they have been allowed to give her medication when she is there, which means that she has some very good days.

Relationship problems

Some service-users enter romantic relations with other people, both other service-users and with people without disorders. This can be really good, but it may also cause a lot of stress if it does not work out.

Marla is 32 years old and has mild intellectual disability. She lives in a group home with nine other people of her age. In a music festival for people with special needs she met Paul who is 35 years old. He lives at another group home in the same municipality. They became a couple.

Fairly soon it turned out that they have two completely different ways of handling setbacks. When they fight (which they do over relatively small disagreements) Marla is afraid the relationship will end. She goes to Paul's group home and demands to talk the fight through with him. She has a big need of reassurance and of the situation being solved quickly.

Paul handles fights by pulling away and does not want to talk to Marla when they have argued. He has a need to be by himself for a while, and when he later on contacts Marla again he pretends that nothing has happened. He finds it really hard to talk about the fight.

Early on in their relationship a pattern was crystallized. After a fight Paul isolated himself. Marla sought him up and refused to go home until they had talked the situation through. Paul hid in his room and pretended not to be at home, but Marla got help from the staff. Finally Paul said: 'Now you must leave, or I'll hit you, and I don't want to do that.' That did not make Marla leave and Paul hit her. She ran home, and after a couple of days Paul contacted her and pretended that nothing had happened.

The relationship was turbulent to say the least; they were both very stressed and lost a lot of quality of life, and after six months Paul was convicted of assaulting Marla. The police report had been filed by the staff at Marla's group home. Paul said: 'She could have just left; I didn't want to hit her.'

What all these basic stress factors have in common is that they are not passing. They remain stress factors for longer periods of time. There may be many more examples and it is up to the reader to come up with more basic stress factors relevant in the lives of the service-users he or she knows.

Situational stress factors

Often we feel that challenging behaviour is triggered by an event. This may be a demand situation or a situation that the service-user cannot survey. Often staff bring up these events in guidance and ask for solutions to these specific situations.

These may be:

- demands
- conflicts
- inability to make others understand
- aches and pains
- sudden noises
- substitute staff
- dislike of staff or other service-users
- sudden changes
- not measuring up
- food
- injustices

- parties
- restraints.

Demands

The staff or the parents think that the service-user is able to manage a certain demand. It may be the demand of taking out the maths book from the bag, going to bed when being told to by the staff, putting on clothes of own accord or getting on the bus at the end of the excursion. It might even be a demand to stop what she is doing.

The service-user reacts to the demand and either refuses or fails to carry it out. The demand is sometimes felt so stressful the service-user cannot do it at once, but must wait until the demand has slightly abated and the service-user has regained control of herself.

Demand situations often lead to challenging behaviour, but we have already dealt with that in the chapter on adjustment of demands. It is not the service-user's fault if challenging behaviour arises in a demand situation.

Conflicts

These may be:

- Conflicts you have a part in yourself. It can be incredibly stressful to some people if somebody is angry with them on the bus. In the same way, being scolded can be very hard. The conflict may however also be more equal, for example the conflicts between Marla and Paul discussed in the previous section.

- Conflicts with other people in your surroundings. This may be how another service-user reacts in a demand situation, but also conflicts between equals. This can be compared to the stress children feel if their parents are fighting. Many people with intellectual disabilities or neuropsychiatric problems are not able to navigate that situation, and cannot predict what is going to happen, which means that other people's conflicts may be difficult to endure.

Inability to make others understand

Communication difficulties often means that you are frustrated in situations where you are trying to make yourself understood. Small children can be very frustrated when they try to communicate and nobody understands, and that is also true for people with different disabilities. To get a punch when you have misunderstood a service-user with poor language is not uncommon working with adults with autism.

Aches and pains

We have all had headaches, toothaches and other passing pains and know what that means for the level of function. As long as we work with people who can express this, we can show necessary consideration, but if we work with service-users without language it is instantly harder.

Sudden noises

Sudden noises can be a great stress to people who generally are sensitive to sensory impressions. A slamming door or a person coughing can be the trigger of challenging behaviour.

Substitute staff

Substitute staff are a well-known stress factor in many educational activities. When I went to school there were two kinds of substitutes:

- those who had not understood that a substitute means a stress to the pupils and therefore tried to teach us from the book

- those who knew that it is difficult to have a substitute and therefore read us stories or played rounders with us.

If a regular school class is sensitive to substitutes, then how much more must it be for our service-users? As a substitute you must relate to being a stress factor and consequently adjust the demands.

Dislike of staff or other service-users

Elsa has a mild intellectual disability. She is 75 years old and lives in a nursing home for elderly people with similar disorders. Elsa has lived in institutions all her adult life. In all these years she has had challenging behaviour, mostly in the form of hitting the staff and throwing furniture. She has had a fit about once a week. Elsa says that sometimes she throws furniture, but only if the staff working with her are ugly.

When Elsa turned 70 she was moving to her present group home. She was not absolutely certain that she wanted to move. When she visited the new group home she asked the manager if the staff were beautiful. The manager asked why. Elsa replied: 'They must be beautiful if they are to work with me, otherwise I sometimes throw furniture.' The manager and Elsa therefore walked around saying hello to the staff, and Elsa told her who she thought was beautiful or ugly.

It turned out that two thirds of the staff were beautiful according to Elsa so the manager said: 'Elsa, I promise you there'll always be one person who is beautiful at the group home, and you will not have to talk to the ugly ones. We make sure that everybody knows who you think should be working with you.' Elsa was pleased and agreed to moving in and she has not thrown any furniture in the five years she has lived there.

There are people Elsa cannot manage being around. She calls them ugly people. Her nephew once asked her if he was beautiful, whereupon Elsa said: 'No, of course not, you're family', so apparently there are three categories in her world. Her conception of beauty has nothing to do with the common conception of beauty. She seems to like certain people whereas others she cannot handle being around. They are simply stressful to her. Her way of describing people she cannot handle being with has unfortunately meant that people have said: 'She's not going to decide who she's going to be with, and at least not based on looks.'

In the same way there are service-users who cannot manage being with certain other service-users. This may be because the other service-user makes annoying sounds or that once a long time ago they had been beaten by the other service-user. This means that when we demand that they are to be in the same room it is hard for our service-user, and we must once again further adjust our demands to make daily life work.

Sudden changes

Sudden changes are perhaps the most common stress factor in people with special needs. We have already discussed the concepts of obstinacy and inflexibility, so it is easy to understand that unpredicted events or changes in daily life could bring anxiety.

> **Adam** is 15 years old and has Asperger's syndrome. He loves Tokio Hotel's music and has been looking forward to their new album. The day of the release of the CD he goes to town to buy it. When he arrives at the store it is not in stock. It has sold out. Adam has not imagined that this could happen so he is very upset. He tells the staff off, calling them incompetent and ignorant of good music, and turns a record stand over.

Adam finds it incredibly hard to deal with changes in daily life, and when there is a change as important as the record store not having the new album by, according to him, the best band in the world, that is too hard for him. He thinks that going to town is hard, but goes because the motivation to obtain the album is big enough. The combined stress of going to town and the stress of the album being out of stock make him experience chaos.

Some changes are made by staff or parents with the best intentions. You feel you are doing something good, without understanding that you ruin a structure and therefore cause stress and anxiety.

> **Camille** lives in a group home for people with autism. She has a great need of predictability in daily life and often checks if the structure is solid. For example, there is a structure that says that her mother comes by to visit twice a week. To check if this agreement is true, Camille sometimes calls her mother and says that she is lonely and wants her to visit her. Her mother wants Camille to be fine and often runs to her car and goes to see Camille. When she arrives at the group home she scolds the

staff and says: 'Now Camille has called me again and told me that she's sad and that you're not doing anything.'

However, Camille cannot deal with her mother coming by, and is clearly stressed that the structure did not hold. She is therefore sad when her mother is there, which means that her mother feels it was good of her to come, which in turn makes her want to go at once next time Camille calls.

The more anxiety Camille has, the more often she calls her mother, which increases her anxiety. We have created a vicious circle where her mother considers herself a knight in shining armour and thinks that the staff are incompetent. The staff, however, are not given the opportunity to work with the structure that has proven to give Camille security as it is interrupted by her mother all the time.

Kevin is 17 years old. He has lived in a group home for children with autism since he was ten. The first few years it worked really well, but in the last couple of years it has become harder. When Kevin moved to the group home all was new and they worked in a very structured way. The staff were trained in TEACCH, but as the years have passed the structure has slid, not least because Kevin has seemed to do fine without it.

The last year has however been hard for Kevin. He feels that he has grown up and worries about what will happen now. Besides, several members of staff have quit and one of those who have worked a lot with Kevin has been on long-term sick leave.

Kevin likes everything that has to do with cars. He enjoys going by car, looking at cars, talking about cars, washing and refuelling cars. Some of his daily structure therefore is about cars.

One day Kevin is feeling quite well; he is happy and alert. After school he and one member of staff go away in the car. The structure says that they are going to the forest for a walk, but Kevin rather wants to go to the car store and look at new cars.

The member of staff thinks that should be OK and during the excursion everything is. Back home Kevin is so restless the staff member brings him to wash the car even though the structure says he should watch TV and then go to bed. Kevin is clearly restless during the car wash and after returning home he begins to slam his head into the wall and scream. The staff call the police who arrive and drive him to psychiatry emergency services where he is admitted and given tranquillizers.

Once again we see that staff have the best intentions of trying to help the service-user, but do not understand what they are doing. First they interrupt the structure because Kevin expresses a wish to go to the car store. It would have been better to make an agreement, that we will do that tomorrow, today we are going to the forest as agreed previously. The result of the change is that Kevin is restless (warning sign). If we are restless ourselves, it may be a good idea to go somewhere and do something nice, so the staff member brings Kevin to the car wash. They forget that Kevin is not ordinary and that the strategies we use for ourselves cannot always be used working with people with developmental disabilities. These two changes from the structure are too much for Kevin and at night he experiences chaos.

In guidance, the staff say that they do not understand why he sometimes gets these outbreaks. They feel that they do everything for him to feel fine. In reality, the responsibility for Kevin's outbreaks lies with the staff and their understanding of what changes mean to a boy like him.

Not measuring up

Many young people have told us that the feeling of being an outsider can be a basic stress factor, but also that when they experience that they are different or cannot manage socially that is a situational stress as well. In the same way, not being able to finish a task they thought they could manage can cause difficulties.

Food

Food is a stress factor for all of us. For example, if the food is really good we need calm, preferably with lit candles and in the company of somebody we feel safe and secure with, if we are truly to enjoy the food. None of us would eat fillet of beef in a hot dog stand. That would not work.

Our service-users are just like anybody else. They are stressed by food. However, what we do to be able to eat good food may not work for them. Eating in company may not be a calming factor; instead social demands may be yet another stress factor to them.

The food situation is often conflict-ridden. There may be demands on sitting and eating properly, which are difficult to live up to when there is food on the table. We usually say that it is easier to learn to eat with a knife and fork if we can practise without food on the plate; the food makes it harder to concentrate on the task.

Injustices

If you are inflexible, injustices often become a palpable problem. This is however easily misunderstood. Perhaps you remember the story about John in chapter two:

John is 12 years old and has Asperger's syndrome and ADHD. He goes to special school. One day a boy of nine years takes his cap at the morning break and runs off with it to his friends. They throw it between them for a few minutes until John manages to get hold of it again.

At the lunch break John goes out with a baseball bat in his hands, finds the nine-year-old playing in the sandpit and hits him with full force in the face. When the staff ask him why he did it he says: 'Then he might learn not to take my cap.' And he probably did.

John tries to remove an imbalance. By removing the imbalance the anxiety is minimized. He has difficulties holding grudges. If he is in conflict with someone and it is solved, he does not hold any grudges.

On the other hand, as long as the imbalance remains it is a huge stress factor to him. He probably has not been able to concentrate in the two classes that have passed between the breaks, but can breathe out after having beaten the nine-year-old. Then the balance is restored and the stress gone.

Parties

Both parents and staff know how hard participating in activities with many people can be to people with developmental disabilities. This is also true for Christmas parties in nursery, in school, in daily life therapy and in bigger group homes. It is also true for city festivals, bigger sports events and concerts. The most common reason for it being hard is that these events are too unpredictable.

> **Emma** is 11 years old and has Asperger's syndrome. She goes to a regular elementary school. It is Elias', one of her classmates, birthday and he has invited the whole class to a party. Emma has had difficulties participating in parties previously and locked herself in the bathroom to get some peace and quiet. She is aware of this, but really wants to go.
>
> Three days before the party Emma calls Elias' mother and asks: 'I'd like to know the programme of the party.' Elias' mother does not quite understand what Emma means, so Emma says: 'Well, I usually find it hard to stay at parties if I don't know the programme so I'd like to know what we're going to eat and when. And then I'd also like to know how many people will be there and when it's over.'

Emma tries to reduce her stress by predictability. To an outsider it might seem a bit strange; most parties for 11-year-olds usually have quite a predictable course of events. But Emma has Asperger's syndrome and consequently has great difficulties generalizing. She has not understood that as most parties happen in a certain way, this one most probably will as well. Besides, she also has difficulties dealing with there being different food in different parties and tries to get an overview by knowing in advance.

Luckily enough, Elias has a kind mother who takes children seriously so Emma got the information she wanted and could go to the party.

Restraints

Restraints have been described by many people I have talked to as the most stressing factor there is. Often the service-user does not know why he or she has been restrained, but describes the experience as the most unpredictable thing they have experienced. The humiliation and powerlessness there is in being restrained have also been difficult to endure, which has increased the anxiety in the situation.

Some people explain that a restraint often has brought a lower self-esteem, less trust to the people around them and more anxiety for long periods of time afterwards.

My stand is that restraints are always unnecessary. Often the situation is provoked by the actions of staff, and this book should give tools to avoid this happening. In rare cases something more may be necessary; we will take a look at this in the next chapter, but as a rule these acts of emergency should be temporary and be based on diversion and relief that give a sense of regaining control of oneself, not on the staff's control of the service-user.

All these situational stress factors are examples. There are many more than these, and some are very individually specific. It is just to help you find those your own service-users have. Of course you should work in a way that does not bring unnecessary situational stress, but you must also remember that some of these may be what renders quality of life. To participate in a Christmas party or a music festival perhaps brings stress, but may also mean wonderful experiences and a memory for life. You must however deal with the level of stress, either by keeping the basic stress factors down or managing the situational ones.

Warning signs

When the collective amount of stress is a little bit too big we often react with different behaviours or have certain symptoms. We can categorize these in different ways: personal warning signs that are particular to the individual; positive warning signs that might appear all bad but have beneficial effects; negative warning signs; and lost skills.

Personal warning signs
WORDS OR SOUNDS
Sometimes these are high singing sounds, sometimes more tic-oriented words or noises, like throat sounds or smacking. Sometimes they are words from certain contexts.

> **Christopher** is ten years old and has ADHD and Asperger's syndrome. He likes the Danish 1970s movies about the Olsen gang. He particularly likes the movie *The Olsen Gang on Track* because it is about a raid on a train.
>
> When he is stressed or the stress is high Christopher may use catch phrases from the movie, for example calling his friends 'You Social Democrat'. He does not do so otherwise.

MOVEMENT PATTERNS
These may include hand or head movements. If a person has tics the greater part of the time because of Tourette's syndrome, the tics often increase in number if he or she is under greater stress than usual.

'DARK EYES'
These are commonly described warning signs by staff. Usually it is a beginning anger that is visible in the eye region.

PARTICULAR FOCUSING ON CERTAIN TOPICS OF CONVERSATION
This may be good or bad for the service-user. Often this is related to feelings of stress or anxiety where some people, particularly those with an intellectual disability, connect the feeling to a specific experience. Therefore they either talk about that experience (for example that Mum died) or what you talked about or did in the very experience.

> **Sandra** is 24 years old and has an intellectual disability. Her parents fought a lot when she was little, and at one time her father hit her mother. This happened while Sandra watched Disney's Christmas Show. Since that day Sandra talks about Disney's

cartoons when she is stressed. She dislikes the cartoons, but they still take up a lot of room in her life.

COMPLEX PERSONAL WARNING SIGNS

These can be very different from person to person. My colleague, Trine Uhrskov, worked with a 21-year-old girl with nonverbal learning disorder who offered the following commentary on our stress factors model: 'Of course I know when I'm under too great stress. That's when I wake up hung over with some guy I don't recognize. When I feel bad I go out to seek appreciation, kiss all kinds of men and have sex with men I don't know.'

Positive warning signs or coping

These signs are actually good as they reduce the stress. The people close to the person do not always find them good, seeing them as problems in themselves, but from the service-user's point of view they have a positive effect, at least in the beginning. Some of them are reminiscent of the strategies for keeping self-control we discussed in chapter two. Positive warning signs include:

- shielding off a stressful daily life
- getting tired and falling asleep
- coping-oriented self-harm
- laziness
- special interests
- imaginary friends
- internet gaming.

SHIELDING OFF A STRESSFUL DAILY LIFE

Some people can shield off mentally, perhaps by not taking in what happens around them. Others need more to be able to shield off, perhaps a computer screen to concentrate on.

Daniel, whom we met earlier on, only manages daily life if he can shield off with the help of TV for a couple of hours every day. He watches American serials and reruns with pleasure. His favourite is *Gilmore Girls*, which perhaps is not an obvious favourite for a 23-year-old man. He says that he relaxes when watching TV, especially if he has seen the show previously. TV also has the advantage of there being a clear structure and that the programme can be kept.

Leo is nine years old and has ADHD. In his first years in school he spent a lot of time outside the classroom, as he could not concentrate and thus was rowdy. In second grade he got a new teacher who thought that this was a problem. He asked Leo: 'Don't you think we should find another way than me being angry with you and sending you out?' Yes, Leo thought so too. 'Then I have a suggestion for you: what do you like to do that can be done in the corridors?' Leo told him that he liked to blow soap bubbles. 'Then I think we should make sure that you get a small wall cupboard in the corridor that only you have the key to. In that locker we put a jar of soap bubbles. When you get unfocused you can go out and blow soap bubbles for five minutes. Is that OK?' Leo thought that five minutes was not enough so they agreed on six minutes instead. Since the day the locker was put up, Leo has gone out of his own accord to blow soap bubbles about once a day, and he has been asked to go out and blow a couple of times a week. He has got a way to shield off and wind down.

Charlie is nine years old and attends special school. Shortly after his school start the teachers discovered that he hid in a TV cabinet when he was stressed. He stayed there for about ten minutes. This happened a couple of times a week in the beginning but now it happens a couple of times a day. When they try to talk to him when he is in the locker he remains silent, and they have not opened the locker while he has been in it. If you try to talk to him about his using the locker he flatly denies doing so. However, a problem has arisen. Charlie has become too big for the locker. At first the teachers cut off a piece of the floor of the cupboard so his bottom stuck out and then it worked for a while, but now he no longer fits; he cannot close the door. The problem is that it may be hard too give him a new hiding place as he will not admit to using it.

These three people use the same coping strategy: they shield off. In that way they are able to manage daily life. Therefore we, in the world around them, should not begin to limit Daniel's TV watching, Leo's bubble blowing or Charlie's locker time.

GETTING TIRED OR FALLING ASLEEP

Newborn babies who are over-stimulated sometimes fall asleep to protect themselves. So do some of our service-users. This could be the reason for pupils in their teens falling asleep in lessons; the stress of being young and the pressure from school may be too much for them.

> **Moa** is 17 years old. She is of average intelligence, but has ADD and autistic traits. When Moa is feeling well she sleeps for ten hours at night and perhaps an hour after school. When she is a little worse she often goes straight to bed after school and only wakes up for dinner. In school she sometimes falls asleep in class.

When Moa sleeps she is not stressed. By sleeping all her spare time, she removes all mental stimuli and demands. She has many demands at school in her daily life, and consequently a lot of sleep is helpful to her. This is not a conscious strategy, but it reduces her stress.

COPING-ORIENTED SELF-HARM

In chapter two when we discussed self-control, we described how some people with an intellectual disability or neuropsychiatric disorders sometimes bite their hand or cut themselves in their arm to manage a difficult situation. The criterion for a self-harm to be coping-oriented is for it to reduce stress in the short term. The behaviour may be:

- biting one's nails or cuticles
- tearing at one's cuticles so small wounds arise
- biting one's hand or arm
- cutting oneself shallowly, most often in one's arm

- pressing or hitting the ulnar nerve
- scratching a wound.

Who can claim to be free of all these behaviours? There is only a difference in levels from tearing at a cuticle when stressed in a queue to cutting oneself in one's arm. Furthermore, many people with neuropsychiatric disorders have a high pain threshold and feel pain in a different way from others. Therefore there is all the more reason to allow this kind of behaviour and, instead of working directly with the behaviour, work on reducing the stress factors that cause it.

LAZINESS

Laziness is perhaps the wrong word as it implies that there is will in the picture. I do not think that will is a relevant concept in this context. People who can behave, will, and if you do not succeed in doing so, you probably simply cannot.

When I was little I was considered lazy. I always tried to find short cuts and get away with doing as little as possible. I always defended myself with it being stupid to make detours and that laziness has pushed the development forward. If we were not lazy by nature, no time- and work-saving inventions would have been made. My laziness was however not particularly popular with teachers and my parents.

In adult life I have realized that the laziness is related to the task. In my teens it was not hard to motivate myself to play the guitar and as an adult it is not hard to lecture, guide staff and write. On the other hand, cleaning the gutters may be a bit harder. If I have had a rough week with a lot of travelling and perhaps a couple of evening lectures, I do not care if the gutters need to be cleared at the weekend. That is done after a calmer week when the stress is lower. There are many youths and adults with intellectual disabilities or neuropsychiatric disorders who are considered lazy. But perhaps that is an excellent way of avoiding stress.

Anton is 22 years old. He got the diagnosis childhood autism when he was three years old, but it was changed to Asperger's syndrome when he was 17. He went to special school in the beginning, but since third grade he has gone to a regular elementary school and later also to a regular secondary school. He has done OK, but not as well as could be expected from his high intelligence.

Anton participates in a self-understanding course where the stress model is used. He says: 'I don't know anything about stress. I'm never stressed. If I feel that something becomes a pressure or that something is difficult I just don't. I back out. If there's too much noise I go home, if an essay stresses me I don't write it. It works perfectly.'

Anton both shields off and gets lazy, and it works for him in the short term. The question is whether it also works in the long run. Perhaps he does not use his full potential, but he has been able to take part in the regular school system and consequently has acquired the basic requirements for college and university. That would perhaps not have been possible if, due to stress, he had been assigned to a special class or special school.

SPECIAL INTERESTS

It is common for people with autism or Asperger's syndrome to develop special interests. It is not uncommon in other disorders either. In autism there is often a sensory point of departure, for example a visual movement or a scent. Aage Sinkbæk, who has Asperger's syndrome, describes that the scent in the beehive is the core of one of his special interests, beekeeping.[*] In severe intellectual disability and autism, they may sometimes be very simple interests like collecting ballpoint pens or handles for tools, while in people with average intelligence they may be very complex interests like opera or wine. In Asperger's syndrome, there is often a technical element in the boys' interests and a social connection in the girls'. The boys perhaps create computer software or like trains while the girls like horses or cats.

Tony Attwood describes special interests as coping strategies. He means that in certain periods you are more focused on your special interests and that this is stress-related. It is consequently not the

---

[*]   Sinkbæk 2002.

special interest in itself that is a warning sign, but the extra focus you may have at times.*

> **Michaela** is 29 years old. She has Asperger's syndrome and is a doctoral student in grammar. Three years ago Michaela met a man, Stephen, and they got married a year later. Stephen is a doctoral student in French, and Michaela says that she likes him very much because he is so good at French.
> Michaela and Stephen recently had a little girl. It has been a tough change for Michaela. She has difficulties handling the fact that her structures are being disrupted by a little girl who does not eat or sleep in a regular pattern. Stephen has had to take on huge responsibility, which he on the other hand certainly likes. Michaela has started seeing a psychologist who helps her create a structure that leaves room for her daughter.
> On the question of what she thinks of when changing nappies and feeding her daughter Michaela answers: 'I think of grammar. Previously I thought of all kinds of things in the day, but now I almost only think of grammar.'

IMAGINARY FRIENDS

Some people make up imaginary friends when they experience something that stresses them a lot. It is not uncommon for three- and four-year-old children to have an imaginary friend if they are going to have a sibling or if the family is moving. Both these types of changes are huge in a small person's life and should therefore be considered great life events. The imaginary friends generally disappear again after a couple of months.

Some imaginary friends, however, do not go away. The basis of this often is that the child has a need for the imaginary friend as a conversation partner to be able to process what is difficult or stressful. Some people with neuropsychiatric disorders or intellectual disabilities keep them for many years.

> **Mary** is 63 years old. She has Down's syndrome. She began her adult life in an institution, but now lives in a group home with her

---

*   Attwood 2006.

own small room where she listens to music and knits. She has great difficulties being with several people at once. She attends daily life therapy.

Mary has 35 imaginary friends. This started in her childhood when she made up an imaginary friend who was a ten-inch tall giraffe. In time this has become 35 giraffes. Mary talks to her giraffes pretty much all the time. It varies how many she brings to work. Sometimes there are three, sometimes ten, and on really bad days she brings them all.

When staff enter Mary's room she cannot always talk to them. Then she talks to the giraffes so they can pass things on to the staff.

Sometimes an imaginary friend develops into something much more complex:

Louise Jensen is 25 years old and lives in Denmark. She has Asperger's syndrome and has among other things made an audiobook with me on social interaction problems.[*] In it she tells that she has a whole world of people in her head that she talks to and partakes in social activities with. She developed this world fairly early on in life, and it was not until she was a teenager that she realized that not everybody has such a world.

She says that it is calming to enter your own world where nothing unpredictable ever happens.

Imaginary friends and own worlds are good. They render it possible to manage a difficult daily life. Therefore there is nothing to worry about as a parent or member of staff. Most people want to be in the real world, but cannot. As soon as they can, they will.

INTERNET GAMING

World of Warcraft (WOW) is a net-based computer game that has become incredibly popular. You play with other gamers from all over the world and to be successful you must cooperate. You communicate through text or speech via the computer.

---

[*]   Hejlskov Jørgensen *et al.* 2005.

Some years ago I got my first case where a boy of 14 years had stopped going to school because he would rather stay at home and play World of Warcraft. Parents and school reacted strongly to this. He was assessed and got the diagnosis Asperger's syndrome. He said that going to school had always been hard. He had no friends and it was difficult managing socially. In the game he had many friends and he often succeeded in what he was doing. In the choice between going to school and staying at home playing, the choice was easy. It gave much more to play than to go to school.

Since then I have met many people with this kind of problem. My experience is that you begin to play because you have difficulties managing socially in real life, but that it is easy in the game. The longer you have been away from school, the harder it is to go there. Then there is a period when parents, school, social services and healthcare are concerned. Is a psychosis about to arise; will he sit there until he is old and dies?

However, after a year or two the boy usually suddenly gets up and out into the world.

Robert started playing WOW when he was 14 years old. When he was 16 he stayed at home playing full-time. He got a social worker, Scott, who was going to try to motivate him to go to school, but it was a difficult task. Robert opened the door every time Scott knocked, but did not want to talk to him for more than five minutes. Sometimes he did not want to talk at all, but played on and said: 'You're welcome to be here, if you must, but you have to let me play in peace and quiet.' When Scott brought sweets or pizza for Robert he declined. He did not want anything from Scott, he said.

After 19 months like this Robert suddenly took the train to go to see a girl 200 miles away he had played with on the net. He came home after a week, but after a few weeks he moved in with her and her parents. Robert's mother was surprised; he had hardly left his room for 19 months and all of a sudden he moved 200 miles away!

After a couple of months Robert contacted Scott. He knew that Scott was team leader at an annual rock festival and wanted to know if Scott could get him and his girlfriend jobs there. Scott was very surprised. Never had he had an assignment with such little work and such great effect, and it even seemed like Robert had formed a relationship with him that he could use.

I believe that young people who quit school to play WOW do so because the anxiety and stress that all youths feel over becoming adults hits them. When it begins to let go they enter the world again. Therefore the people close to the person should be careful of setting too much pressure, which could make it difficult for them to get back into the world when it is time. Suddenly it is no longer the young person's own travels into the world, but the mother's or psychologist's. Robert was lucky to be able to get out into the world with his girlfriend at her parents. That would perhaps not have been possible at home.

NEGATIVE WARNING SIGNS

Negative warning signs are common, not only in people in the field of special education, but in all of us. They are negative because they often increase the stress instead of reducing it. They include:

- irritability and aggressiveness
- insecurity and anxiety
- infections
- stomach pains
- sensory sensitivity
- sleep disorders
- compulsive thoughts and behaviour
- mood swings
- restlessness
- depression and pessimism
- lack of surplus
- reduced learning ability.

IRRITABILITY AND AGGRESSIVENESS

Irritability and aggressiveness perhaps are those warning signs that most often cause problems to the people around the person, and are in many people's opinion also synonymous with challenging behaviour. Therefore irritability and aggressive behaviour cause negative feedback to the service-user, which consequently increases the stress. They are, however, very obvious warning signs, and if you as a person close to the service-user can handle his or her aggression and do not take it personally, you can use it to navigate. With aggression, you must reduce the stress level and adjust your demands better.

INSECURITY AND ANXIETY

In my book, anxiety is a greater problem than aggression. Anxiety limits people in many more ways and causes much worse quality of life.

> **Sam,** who has ADHD and autistic traits, was hit in the head by a rock when he was eight years old. The rock was thrown by another boy, but was not meant for Sam. He was incredibly scared and had anxiety over getting rocks in the head for a full year after the event.
>
> When Sam went to secondary school he experienced quite high pressure. He was very ambitious and also did well, but it cost him a lot of work. He started getting anxiety attacks, hyperventilated, got palpitation, dizziness and was sweating. Sam has fairly big difficulties with central coherence, which meant that he related the anxiety to the old incident with the rock. When he had an anxiety attack he thought he had been hit with a rock in his head. He even began to ask his classmates if they had seen the rock he had just been hit by and asked if he was bleeding.
>
> Sam's parents and teachers began to think that he was about to fall into a psychosis as they assumed that his talk about rocks was a serious thinking disorder. He therefore started seeing a psychologist, who fairly soon understood that he connected anxiety to the old event.

> She started working with his understanding of how anxiety is felt in the body and the anxiety attacks went away. At the same time Sam's stress was reduced; the anxiety attacks had increased his stress levels considerably.

Anxiety can be disabling in relation to social intercourse. Some people who develop anxiety limit their social relations in order to limit the risk of getting anxious when with other people. They isolate themselves at home. Unfortunately, anxiety often increases when you isolate yourself, as you do not feel that you are doing well when defying your anxiety. This means that from having been a warning sign the anxiety is suddenly the greatest basic stress factor. I therefore think that if anxiety begins to take over a person's life, it should be treated either medically or with targeted cognitive psychotherapeutic methods. It is not only a treatment of symptoms, but also a treatment of something that soon can turn into a considerable stress factor.

INFECTIONS

Infections and viral attacks as a result of stress have been known for many years. Today it is believed that the immune system deteriorates when you are under stress. Among other things, it has been shown that you get the flu more often if you are under stress and that wounds heal 49–60 per cent more slowly in a stressed period than in a calm. Even John Cleese from Monty Python has written about his stress and how he through conversational therapy got help to keep it down and consequently keep his constant infections at bay.[*]

This does not mean that all infections are the result of stress, but that we are more sensitive to infections if we are under pressure. This is true for all people, not only our service-users.

---

[*] Kiecolt-Glaser *et al.* 2005; Lazarus 1999; Marucha, Kiecolt-Glaser and Favagehi 1998; Skynner and Cleese 1993; Smolderen *et al.* 2007.

STOMACH PAINS

Stomach pains are a well-known warning sign that is often related to anxiety and discomfort in children. In adults they are often related to gastric catarrh that can be the result of psychological stress.

In extreme cases when the body is under maximal stress, for example burns, head injuries or blood poisoning, stress-related bleeding gastric ulcers can suddenly arise. On the other hand, 'ordinary' ulcers are believed to be infections caused by a bacterium, *H. pylori*, which does not, however, mean that pains cannot increase under stress because of the deterioration of the immune defence. It could still be a combination of stress and bacterial infection.[*]

SENSORY SENSITIVITY

Sound, light and other sensory sensitivities are common in people with special needs, both in the neuropsychiatric field and in intellectual disability or brain damage. This does not mean necessarily that the sensitivity is constant. I earlier described this kind of difficulty as a basic stress factor; the warning sign is that the difficulties increase. You become more sensitive and it is even harder to screen your impressions.

This is not only true for our service-users, but also for ourselves. If we are in a hurry to get to a meeting and cannot find a parking space but have to drive around, we turn off the car stereo. We are sensitive to sensory impressions when we are under pressure. You must be able to manage this when working with people with special needs; that the service-user is able to be in a certain environment on a good day does not mean that he or she can manage it on a bad day. And unfortunately you cannot turn off noise from the surroundings in the same way as you turn off the car stereo.

Increased sensitivity increases the overall stress level. Therefore increased sensitivity is a negative warning sign.

SLEEP DISORDERS

We have all experienced having our sleep ruined by stress. If something difficult happens in life, like a death in your family or you

---

[*]   Feldman 2002; Kleibeuker and Thijs 2004.

lose your job, you often have problems sleeping for several nights afterwards. You can lie awake because of financial problems, love problems, your children's diseases or worry about world peace. We have all tried to make the day work after a sleepless night. It rarely goes well. Therefore sleep disorders are a negative warning sign; they often increase the stress.

It is like this for our service-users as well. Some of them already have sleep disorders because of their neuropsychiatric problems. For them the warning sign is that the sleep disorders worsen.

COMPULSIVE THOUGHTS AND BEHAVIOUR

Compulsive thoughts and compulsive behaviours are more common than you might immediately think. If you ask a group of people whether anyone has a compulsive behaviour, not many raise their hands. If on the other hand you ask whether there is anyone who does not have a compulsive behaviour, no one raises their hands. We probably all have compulsive behaviours on and off, at least when we are under pressure. Of course we all double-check windows, the cooker, the iron and the coffee machine before going away for a holiday, but not usually before we go to work.

An older acquaintance of mine, **Anthony**, has three locks on his door. Once someone was going to water his flowers when he was at his holiday home. When he was away the person watering the flowers locked all the three locks that she had been given keys to. That meant that Anthony could not get in when he came home, because he had only brought keys to two of the locks. He said: 'When I'm in town I only lock one lock. If I'm going to the country I lock two. It's only when I'm abroad that I lock all the three locks.' It was not how long he would be away, but only how well-known the situation was or how far away he was going that determined how many locks were necessary for him not to worry.

Per Johnson, a lecturer at Lund University, once said that compulsive thoughts are common. He offered the thought 'I'm too fat' as the most common compulsive thought in Western society. So we all probably have compulsive thoughts too on and off.

Both compulsive behaviour and compulsive thoughts increase when we are under pressure.

Nicholas has Asperger's syndrome. He is 25 years old and has a charity-funded job in the computer trade. Nicholas has a specific phobia of bridges. He lives in Denmark where it is hard to manage without bridges, both big and small. However, he is able to cross bridges by foot or car, but it is a little scary.

Once Nicholas went home with me from a conference on Asperger's syndrome. When we crossed the Great Belt Fixed Link Nicholas was very stressed. He was sweating and checked if he had his mobile phone and keys in his pocket all the time. When we were back on safe ground everything was fine again.

Just before we arrived in Copenhagen we crossed another bridge, and he was once again stressed. Only a few minutes later the road goes over a low bridge which you do not notice unless you know of it. Nicholas was calm until he suddenly took a quick look on either side of the road and realized that there was water on both sides. He immediately started feeling his pockets to see that keys and mobile phone were where they should.

Nicholas's compulsive behaviour is not uncommon and not obvious to the people around him, if you do not as we did sit in a car for several hours. It is not disabling in daily life either, so he does not need another diagnosis. It is however a warning sign both to Nicholas and the people around him and is connected with certain anxiety, therefore we consider it a negative warning sign.

In the same way, we worry more about our weight when we are under pressure and that increases our anxiety.

MOOD SWINGS

Mood swings are also a known sign of stress and a warning sign in psychotic problems. I have encountered it in many contexts in my work and experienced many people's frustration over it. It is hard to plan a day if you are to leave room for a service-user's mood swings. All too happy is not necessarily good; it can, in connection with mood swings, entail sudden emotional changes for the least reason. This sets very high demands on the staff's ability to adjust demands.

RESTLESSNESS

Restlessness is perhaps recognizable from your own life. If you have many things to do or if you have a long essay or the like to write, you are often restless before you actually get started. You may even be restless to such an extent that you do not get started at all but do all kinds of other things – cleaning, washing up, surfing the net, etc. However, you do not get what you are supposed to do done, and the pressure increases the more time you waste.

Our service-users may not always start doing the dishes, but motor unrest is not uncommon at all. It keeps the adrenaline levels high, which does not contribute to feeling calm.

Sometimes the restlessness makes the service-user want to have contact with or feedback from other people. This is mostly true for service-users who have outgoing personalities. Some service-users in that situation become very talkative and contact seeking, others pinch or are verbally confronting. It is very easy to be drawn into a conflict by a stressed service-user, and the stress usually spreads to the others. This is particularly hard if you work with people with attention disorders. I have often met people with ADHD who have got a faulty borderline diagnosis because they reacted in a borderline way when under pressure.

In all these situations it is important to work calmly and methodically and create a structure around the service-user at the same time as you focus on the perspective. But you must make sure that you are able to keep your own calm. Which is not always that easy.

DEPRESSION AND PESSIMISM

Many of those I meet in my work have developed depressive traits in their childhood. It is not that strange, because if you have neuropsychiatric problems or an intellectual disability there are many things in life you will not succeed doing and you experience many defeats in life. Psychiatrist Mohammad Ghaziuddin estimates that 30 per cent of all people with Asperger's syndrome suffer from depression at a given time, and similar numbers have also been mentioned for the other diagnoses that require average intelligence. How many people with special needs experience a depression sometimes in their life is not easy to say, but according to Tony Attwood it is not uncommon,* which accounts with my own experience. Ghaziuddin, however, means that the number is true both for people of average intelligence and for people with intellectual disabilities, but that it is harder to diagnose if the developmental level is low.**

The slighter form, pessimism, I often see in social club activities for youths with Asperger's syndrome. It sometimes leads to a negative attitude towards life, negative expectations in other people and a relatively low self-esteem.

If daily life, both in educational activities and spare time is good, self-esteem may be OK, perhaps with a setback now and then. If there are difficulties, it is good to know and adjust accordingly. Then you can limit low self-esteem to the areas where there are difficulties.

Sometimes, however, you see that self-esteem has sunk in general. The service-user has become despondent and pessimistic and perhaps even anxiety ridden. That is usually a sign of there being something not working in school, at work or in spare time, and we must get in and adjust the educational or care frame. This is particularly obvious in work with children and young people who are included in mainstream schools despite special needs. To put it simply, the warning signs about self-esteem are good to use to make sure that the pupil always has a good enough life.

Albin is 18 years old. When he was little he had the diagnosis autism, but developed so well that as a 13-year-old he was instead diagnosed with Asperger's syndrome. The development has continued and today he seems quite ordinary to many people. This unfortunately means that you often forget that he has special needs.

Albin goes to secondary school, where he is taking an arts programme with a musical direction. He plays the piano, both classical and contemporary music. In secondary school he has had more and more social defeats and feels very lonely. At the same time the pressure to manage his subjects in school increases and he worries about what will happen after secondary

---

*   Attwood 2008.

**   Ghaziuddin 2005.

school. He is anxious and afraid that he will be alone when he moves away from home and thinks that it is difficult to make contacts with and build relationships with the opposite sex.

His solution is not to bother with what he finds difficult, in both school subjects and relationships, and he isolates himself more and more. He even stops practising the piano. He says: 'There is no point in anything; everything's going to go to hell for me anyway.'

LACK OF SURPLUS

A lack of surplus is not uncommon if you are under high stress. We have all slept badly and felt that the surplus has been low the following day. This may be positive if you use it as a reason for taking it easy, but often neither our service-users nor we have that possibility. In chapter one, I discussed what the surplus means in relation to the ability to do what is right. Similarly, we also know by experience what a bad job you may do if you do not have the energy required.

Lack of surplus can be visible in relation to school, work or daily life therapy, behaviour, when spending time with friends or taking part in other social contexts.

REDUCED LEARNING ABILITY

Learning ability both regarding learning of skills and of knowledge can be affected by stress. This does not mean that reading difficulties or mathematical difficulties can be explained from a perspective of stress; the proofs of heredity are too comprehensive. But since it means learning ability reduces when under pressure, for people with reading or mathematical difficulties it means that the learning capacity is further reduced.

The same is true for knowledge learning; we learn less from our experiences and from reading or teaching if we are under stress. This is another reason to adjust demands; you learn more if the demands are adjusted according to your surplus than if a teacher puts pressure above the pupil's ability.*

Lost skills

Lost skills constitute another type of warning sign – but one that neither helps nor harms. They are therefore neither positive nor negative. Some of them have been recognized since Nuechterlein and Dawson formulated their model in the 1980s; others are specific to the field of special needs. All are about losing a skill you normally have, and getting it back when you are well again. You lose skills in areas where you have difficulties slightly faster and more often than in areas where you have no problems.

HYGIENE AND ORDER

This warning sign is a true classic. Some psychiatrists I have talked to use the expression 'psychosis hair' about the hairdo you get if you have not washed or combed your hair for a fairly long time so it is like a clod at the back of your head. This usually happens when a patient is on her way into a psychotic period.

Hygienic problems can take many other forms than psychosis hair. This is not about losing the ability to manage your own hygiene, whether it is washing of clothes, body care or tooth brushing, but rather the surplus to get it done and the understanding of how important it is.

A milder variant of this is the ability to keep order. This can be cleaning your house, keeping order on your desk, in the fridge or your economy, or even keeping a pile of letters, bills or other important papers in order. Perhaps leaflets or other unimportant things sneak into the pile if you are under extra high stress for a period of time, and suddenly you are late paying a bill as you have forgotten that it was in the pile.

These warning signs are mostly seen in people who have responsibility for their own hygiene and order. There may, however,

---

*   Lueti, Meier and Sandi (2008); Sandi and Pinelo-Nava 2007; Schumacher *et al.* 2007; Shalev *et al.* 2001.

be examples that a child's lacking hygiene is a warning sign of the parents' stress.

ABILITY TO CREATE STRUCTURES

The ability to create structures is coherent with the ability to keep order. This is, however, about the ability to arrange your time or your surroundings according to a system. This may be making the morning routines work so you have the time to do what you should, being on time by estimating how long a course of events takes, or packing your suitcase when you are going away.

People with difficulties creating structures at all may do fine if everything around them is calm, but as soon as the stress increases everything falls apart and their whole life is chaotic.

LANGUAGE ABILITIES

It is not uncommon for all of us to get linguistic problems when we are under pressure. We may sometimes search for a word a little longer than usual, or our language is imprecise. I live with both Danish and Swedish in daily life, which means that in periods of higher stress than usual I have difficulties keeping the languages apart and start using expressions from one of the languages in the other.

People with linguistic difficulties, which are very common in our service-user group, lose their linguistic skills more often than others and sometimes so much that their language is lost. They may be forced to use other forms of communication and begin to lean on body language or communicate with screaming, invectives, simple threats or violence.

Some service-users, those with autism or Asperger's syndrome, among others, sometimes have a need to be assisted by written messages, even if they normally do not, because the spoken language does not work in a stressed situation.

PRESENCE

We have all experienced having too little surplus to take part in social intercourse. Perhaps you come home from an extra tough day at work and find it hard to be present to your children or partner. Sometimes you are strained in another way, perhaps by poisoning the body with alcohol the night before an elderly relative's birthday, which could mean that the ability to be active and present at the party is reduced.

Our service-users have the same experiences, but perhaps slightly more often. This may be related to the previously discussed positive warning sign to shield off mentally.

SOCIAL SKILLS

Social skills are about the ability to read and relate to other people's social signals. They can also be about the ability to contact other people in an ordinary and socially accepted way and to stay out of conflicts. For ordinary people in pressed periods of time, this may show by you finding it hard to know how far you should go when teasing other people or that you miss subtle social signals and are worse at reading social situations.

A great part of our service-users have fairly major difficulties in the social field, which means that there is a risk of the social skills disappearing completely when under pressure.

Matthew is 22 years old. He has Asperger's syndrome, but his difficulties are not that pronounced. Matthew is a happy boy who has his own flat and studies applied systems science at university. He likes to program and he enjoys hard rock. He has long hair and wears black clothes.

Matthew has many friends and is well liked in his circle of friends. He often goes for coffee with his friends, but bigger events are usually too much for him. He says himself that he is stressed by being with too many people at once.

Nevertheless, one night he goes to a concert with a group of friends, four boys and three girls. After the concert one of the girls takes Matthew aside and asks him if he wants to go to her place and watch a movie she has just bought, *Matrix*. Matthew says: 'No, I've already seen that.' Not until later, when he is alone in his flat, does it hit him that she may have had other things than movie watching on her mind.

Washid is 25 years old and has ADHD. He manages life fairly well. He works at a pizzeria where he delivers pizzas. At one time he buys not only a TV and a stereo, but also a computer on credit and suddenly feels he has difficulties paying his bills. This stresses him. One day he also has very much to do at work and even has problems finding an address. When he finally gets there the customer complains loudly about the pizza having gone cold and demands a new pizza. Washid is a kind man and usually is good at taking the customers' complaints. Today however it is too much; he does not know how to handle the situation but is angry and punches the customer.

CONCENTRATION

The standard situation with the car keys gone missing is related to this warning sign. In a stressed situation how often have we looked for the car keys even though we had them in our hands only a minute ago? Then we find them in the fridge or in another similarly weird place. This never happens when we have peace and quiet. This is because when we are in a hurry we cannot concentrate enough to keep our mind on the car keys.

MEMORY

Memory works in the same way as concentration. If we are to remember to call the car mechanic or the plumber it should preferably be on a calm day. If there are too many deviations from daily life, we cannot do it, and if there are too many stress factors, we cannot either. We are simply too distraught when we are under pressure.

SCHOOL SKILLS

School skills that disappear for a period of time is another well-known sign of a high level of stress. I have talked to teachers who describe pupils in regular elementary school who cannot do division on days they are moving between divorced parents, but can do it all other days. One teacher told me about a pupil who stubbornly insisted on never having come across division before, despite attending sixth grade and having used it previously.

EVERYDAY SKILLS

Everyday skills can also disappear for a period of time. I have previously brought up the example of the pupils who could not tie their shoes after a gym class, perhaps because their adrenaline levels were too high. Other everyday skills may also disappear when experiencing a high level of stress, for example cooking, using the computer or going shopping on your own.

ABILITY TO ACT STRATEGICALLY

The ability to find good strategies for action may also disappear if you are under stress. These can be about flexibility or imagination. Many people have a tendency to repeat behaviour in stressed periods instead of coming up with new strategies. This also means that the readiness of your thinking and the open-mindedness for new ways of thinking or acting are reduced.

Warning signs can be excellent tools to use for adjusting care work to the specific service-user. Therefore it may be a good idea to map out every service-user's warning signs. Some warning signs are reminiscent of challenging behaviour, which is not that strange if we set out from the idea that people who can behave also will. The reason for not behaving may simply be a current high stress level. By seeing it as a warning sign and not challenging behaviour we also move the focus from what service-users should change about themselves to what we can do to change the service-user's needs for managing their daily life. By doing so we get the power to influence not only the service-user's life but also our own as staff or parents.

Signs of chaos

There are two types of signs of chaos: the acute and the long-lasting. Acute signs of chaos arise when the stress in a given situation crosses the chaos limit. Most of these signs of chaos are short and temporary, but often painful to the service-user. In the situation of chaos the service-user has no self-control and therefore can't do much about his or her behaviour; and he or she is often so confused that he or she can't sort out what happened when you try to talk the situation through afterwards.

Violent challenging behaviour

Much of what is normally considered violent challenging behaviour belongs to the acute chaos. These include:

- acting-out behaviour

- anxiety attacks and panic attacks

- impulsive suicide attempts

- violent self-harm.

ACTING-OUT BEHAVIOUR

This is the kind of chaos experience I am most often asked to help staff manage. The reason for this is that acting-out behaviour is a problem for the staff (you may get a beating), while other kinds of chaos, like anxiety are primarily a problem for the service-user. The types we most often see are:

- Hits, head-butts, kicks and bites – these behaviours are rarely particularly complicated or refined. Often it is about a hit from above with an open hand, bites on the arms or the front of the body or kicks from a short distance. This means that it is not that hard to protect oneself. We will get into how to manage this type of behaviour in the next chapter.

- Screaming – this can be lengthy and incredibly strenuous for the people around the person.

- Tearing one's clothes apart – in activities for people with intellectual disabilities or severe autism this is common. Some people continue until they are naked, after which they are able to calm down. Then the tearing of clothes has a natural ending and they can collect themselves again. Other people only tear a t-shirt or the like apart.

- Damage – this is often in the form of throwing things around. The standard situation is when crockery is thrown on the ground in a quarrel, but service-users who throw furniture or other things around are also very common. Sometimes they wreck their own things and are sad when the chaos has passed.

Ricky is 35 years old and has Down's syndrome and intellectual disability. He is sometimes very upset if something turns out not to be as expected. In those cases he usually expresses loud sounds and looks around for something to throw. The staff have therefore developed a method: when Ricky starts with his high sounds they throw him a towel. This he grabs and throws around for a few minutes until he calms down.

ANXIETY ATTACKS AND PANIC ATTACKS

Under this heading I refer to anxiety attacks and panic attacks of a more violent form than those considered as warning signs.

Gabriel started school at the local elementary school. In nursery he proved to have difficulties with certain social activities. It was assumed that he would do better in school, as there it would not only be about being able to play, but also very much about learning, an area where he had no known difficulties. He was, on the contrary, very eager to learn and had wide knowledge in the most diverse subjects. He was often described as somewhat precocious.

The first week in school Gabriel was anxious. He had difficulties managing the social interplay and was by himself during breaks. In class he was silent and careful. In the following weeks he was still alone at the breaks, but began to take part in the schoolwork. He did not raise his hand, but did his tasks and kept to himself.

After a couple of weeks the teacher noticed that Gabriel was starting to take quite a long time to get started. He did not get his books out of his bag and often sat fiddling with his pencil or eraser. When she asked him to take out his things, he became anxious but managed to get them out.

When Gabriel had gone to school for a month the teacher was annoyed with him. How come she always had to remind him personally about everything she had already told the class? She told him off and he was terrified. He sat under his desk and soiled his pants. Then he cried heartbreakingly until his mother came and fetched him.

This was repeated at even intervals the entire first term and caused an assessment of Gabriel at a child psychiatry clinic. He was diagnosed with Asperger's syndrome.

Gabriel's anxiety was violent. I have worked quite a lot with different people with this kind of strong anxiety that may be apparent by:

- panic anxiety attacks where the heart rushes and you get dizzy from hyperventilation – you are often afraid you are going to die

- violent anxiety experiences with incontinence, sweating and hallucinations – the anxiety is often diffuse in this kind of anxiety experience so you do not know what you are afraid of.

Both types are terrifying and mean a lot of suffering for the people experiencing them.

IMPULSIVE SUICIDE ATTEMPTS

Trying to jump from a window, throwing yourself in front of a car or taking whatever medicine is available are examples of behaviour not uncommon in people of average intelligence with neuropsychiatric disorders, but which is rarely successful. If you are experiencing chaos, you do not have the ability to structure, plan or execute a suicide.

Ellen is 19 years old. She has some difficulties with attention, social skills and managing nonverbal information. Her difficulties are in the field often denoted NLD (nonverbal learning disability). Ellen has been living for a couple of years in a student home on weekdays and goes to a secondary school for pupils with special needs.

At the student home they work with structure as a basis, which Ellen finds a bit hard. She does not manage to remain seated until everyone has finished eating, and she finds the reprimands she gets from the staff difficult. When it is too much for her, she goes out to the road and throws herself in front of cars or tries to jump out the window.

In the last three years, she has made several hundred suicide attempts of this kind, but they have only resulted in a few visits to the hospital; the cars have managed to stop in time and the student home is situated on the ground floor. Ellen has not made a single suicide attempt at home where she is at the weekends. By adjusting the demands at the student home her suicide attempts disappeared completely.

VIOLENT SELF-HARM

This often differs from coping-oriented self-injury by not being calming. Often it is about slamming one's head into the wall or floor, but it can also involve more complex behaviours.

> **Dennis** is 42 years old. He has autism and a long history of self-injurious behaviour. He uses coping-oriented self-harm by scraping his arms and shinbones with hard objects and scratching himself with his nails. When he experiences chaos his self-injurious behaviour is violent. He breaks windows to cut himself deeply on the glass shards or finds pointy sticks to push into his stomach.

Violent self-harm does not have to have a connection to other self-injury, but can arise from nothing in a situation of chaos.

> **Agnes** is 22 years old. She had ADHD and since she was 17 has developed schizophrenia. In one of her fairly regular stays on a psychiatric ward, her medication is changed. She starts to get side effects she has not had before, and a doctor says that the medication may not be good for her. She therefore begins to refuse taking the medicine. One night the nurse comes to Agnes with her evening medicine. She refuses to take it and asks why she cannot have another medicine now when she gets these side effects. The nurse says in a surly tone: 'If you don't want to take the medicine, then why are you here?' Agnes, who has never before had any self-injurious behaviour, quickly slams her head into the wall three times. On being asked why she did so, she replies: 'It was just that she wasn't kind at all and I couldn't

take it.' This situational stress factor trigged Agnes' first and so far only self-harm incident.

Non-violent challenging behaviour

Some signs of chaos are less violent, but are not felt less frightening to the person experiencing them. These include:

- disorientation
- inability to act
- loss of reality.

DISORIENTATION

Disorientation or confusion is perhaps the most common sign of chaos. This can happen to anyone.

Nicky was visiting England to attend a training course. The course leader was an Englishman called Rob. The evening of the first day the group went out to eat and then went to a pub. Nicky has a rule that usually helps him not to drink too much, namely not to drink more than the person next to him. Unfortunately, he was seated next to Rob.

After a fairly wet night, Nicky was feeling quite bad the next morning. He still arrived for the course, but after half an hour he was sent back to the hotel. It simply did not work. He later said: 'I went out to get a taxi. It was raining a lot, which was quite tough. When I came to the road the cars were driving on the wrong side. I simply had no idea how to get a taxi or how to get back to the hotel. Being in another country isn't easy, and being hung over is a huge stress to the whole system. The rain and the cars driving on the wrong side for me to wave for a taxi was simply too much. I stood in the rain for an hour before figuring out how to do it.'

Nicky experienced chaos, but did not react with acting-out behaviour or other challenging behaviour, though he was disoriented enough for it to take an hour to collect himself. The stress factors piled up until the level of chaos was met and he lost his orientation.

This often happens to our service-users as well, and sometimes is related to the next sign of chaos.

INABILITY TO ACT

The inability to act usually takes the form of a short-term inability to take any kind of initiative.

> **Jonah** is 16 years old. He has no diagnosis and has gone to a regular elementary school all his life. He is good at maths and physics and loves biology. He does really well in school and has for many years competed with a girl in class who is the best pupil in the science subjects. When they were 15 years old they became an item. Jonah says that they can talk about anything and that they like the same things and have a great time together.
>
> After the new year in ninth grade, when Jonah is turning 16, his maths and physics teacher is injured in a traffic accident and he gets a new teacher. At the same time his English teacher goes on maternity leave.
>
> The first school day after the Christmas holidays he gets the news of the maths teacher's accident and only sees substitute teachers. At the same day at lunch his girlfriend breaks up with him, his first girlfriend, who he also describes as his soulmate and the first person he feels he can understand and who understands him. The relationship lasted nine months.
>
> After school he goes home, enters the sitting room and stands in the middle of the floor. He is still standing there when his mother comes home from work three hours later. She gets him into bed and he stays home from school for a week. After that he begins to develop a number of compulsive behaviours, which he never had before. The family contacts a psychologist for cognitive treatment, and in four months the compulsive behaviours are gone and he is well again.
>
> Jonah gets no diagnosis, but the psychologist and he reach the conclusion that he has certain autistic traits that may have added to the development of the compulsive behaviours or at least to the experience of chaos.

Compulsive behaviour has previously been described as a warning sign. Here the experience of chaos comes first, and then the warning signs take over when the stress decreases. Jonah is now 20 years old and describes how he can control his level of stress with the help of his compulsive behaviour; if he begins to get a compulsive feeling he turns down the stress, until the feeling goes away.

LOSS OF REALITY

Losing a sense of reality or psychotic episodes are not at all uncommon. Some young people with neuropsychiatric disorders I have talked to say that they at several times have experienced standing by watching themselves from the outside. This is called *dissociation* in psychiatric terminology and is considered a quite serious psychotic symptom. In a group of young people that I taught on a self-understanding course for people with Asperger's syndrome, over one third had experienced this, often in relation to examinations.

Other psychotic symptoms I have encountered are short-lived, single hallucinations. These can be visual, auditory or scent hallucinations, or experiences of something crawling on your body.

> **Thomas** has ADHD. Since he was little he has had a strong phobia of spiders. In his late teens he was quite under pressure at school and worried about how he would manage life. Several times he felt big clusters of spiders hanging down from gutters or rolling down the wall. The experiences were fairly short-lived, and he knew they were hallucinations.

Experiences of this kind do not have to be early schizophrenia, but are often single psychotic episodes. They arise when you are under massive pressure. This type of experience has often been reported by soldiers in combat.

What these non-violent behaviours have in common is that they render an experience of chaos such that you lose the ability to influence your life. There may be much frustration in the situation of chaos itself, but also anxiety afterwards: could it happen again, and is there any possibility of exerting an influence if and when it happens again? In the chaos situation you have no self-control at all, and that is a very frightening experience.

There are also signs of chaos that arise after stress over a long period of time. It is these that are described in Nuechterlein and Dawson's original model, and we have added another few that we have seen. These signs of chaos arise slowly, which means that we do not always connect them to stress, but we have seen that if you work on the level of stress the symptoms are reduced. They are often described as psychiatric diseases or comorbid psychiatric problems.[*]

It is commonly assumed that psychiatric supplementary problems arise from interaction with the world around the person, and there are indications that the sensitivity for influence from the environment is higher in groups with neuropsychiatric problems than in the rest of the population.[**] This means that the risk of developing behavioural problems or psychiatric diseases is higher in our service-users, but also that our role is more important than we might think. We can influence the quality of life of our service-users, not just here and now, but also in time if we can prevent the development of psychiatric supplementary problems and behaviour problems.[***]

---

[*]   In different contexts, these kinds of problem have been described as more common in people with neuropsychiatric disorders or intellectual disabilities. For example, Ghaziuddin, Weidmer-Mikhail and Ghaziuddin (1998) found that 65 per cent of their group of patients with Asperger's syndrome had symptoms of mental disease. Kessler *et al.* (2006) found in a big population study (National Comorbidity Survey Replication Study) that in the groups with the diagnoses depression, bipolar disorder and anxiety disorder 32, 21 and 9.5 per cent respectively had ADHD. Sukhodolsky *et al.* (2008) found anxiety disorder in 43 per cent of a group of 171 children with pervasive developmental disorders. Linna *et al.* (1999) found psychiatric problems in 32.5 per cent of a group of school children with intellectual disabilities. Merrick (2005) found that 46 per cent of all people with intellectual disabilities who lived at group homes in Israel received neuroleptic medication daily, while Spreat, Conroy and Jones (1997) found that 22 per cent of all adults with a known intellectual disability in Oklahoma, USA, also received it.

[**] Hamilton, Sutherland and Iacono (2005) have shown that stress in the form of life events is important for the development of supplementary problems in people with mild intellectual disabilites, while it means less in people with severe intellectual disabilities. This probably has to do with the experience and understanding of a life event, for example the death of a parent, than with resilience against stress.

[***] Caspi *et al.* 2002; Caspi and Moffitt 2006; Maughan 1995; Moffitt 2005.

Long-term chaos signs

Enough of the acute chaos signs. We will move on to the long-lasting warning signs of chaos, which include:

- depression
- psychoses
- eating disorders
- anxiety states.

DEPRESSION

Depression is perhaps the most common chaos sign. It may, however, be hard to recognize in certain groups, especially in people with serious language difficulties. However, many of the common cognitive symptoms of depression are rare in people with intellectual disability. Instead, they are apparent by sleep disorders, appetite disorders, irritability, mood swings and challenging behaviour.

It is widely accepted among researchers and clinics that depression is quite common in the field of special education; among other things Ghaziuddin estimates that 30 per cent of all adults with Asperger's syndrome are depressed.[*]

Colleagues of mine who work a lot with adults with Asperger's syndrome often even say that it is hard to say whether a certain symptom is a symptom of Asperger's or depression as most adults with Asperger's syndrome have symptoms you in other people normally consider symptoms of depression.

PSYCHOSES

Psychoses that are not fleeting passing episodes are perhaps not as common as depression in our group of service-users, but are on the other hand the standard sign of chaos in the diathesis-stress model (see Figure 4.1). Several studies have shown that people with an

---

[*]   Adewuya and Famuyiwa (2007) found that more than 20 per cent of children with ADHD had depression. Stewart *et al.* (2006) established that the greater part of a group of people with Asperger's syndrome and autism had depression. Hurley, Folstein and Lam (2003) found that depression was the most common psychiatric disease in people with mild intellectual disability. See also Attwood 2008; Ghaziuddin 2005; Smiley and Cooper 2003.

intellectual disability have a three to ten times greater risk of getting a psychosis compared to the population at large.[*]

In severe intellectual disability and autism we often use medicines developed for the treatment of psychosis and schizophrenia (so-called neuroleptica) to reduce challenging behaviour and violent self-injury.[**] In ADHD and Tourette's syndrome these medicines are used when central nervous system stimulants do not have the desired effect on the behaviour. We must therefore assume that a fairly large proportion of our service-users have psychotic problems at times.

The theory behind the development of schizophrenia is that there is a genetic predisposition that does not itself trigger the disease. It is not until the person has been under pressure for some time that the first psychosis is triggered. Through medication in combination with reducing the stress and teaching good coping strategies you can in many cases avoid further psychotic episodes.

The pressure that triggers schizophrenia is often related to adolescence, which is why schizophrenia most often first appears at that time, but it has also been shown that soldiers under long-term pressure can develop similar symptoms. In the diathesis-stress model, Nuechterlein and Dawson describe the genetic predisposition as a vulnerability that determines where the limit of psychosis is.

Our experience in Sweden and Denmark is that in some institutions catering for adults with autism or intellectual disabilities neuroleptica are not used at all, while in others up to a third of the adult service-users are in medical treatment with different kinds of antipsychotic medication.

EATING DISORDERS

Eating disorders are not uncommon in neuropsychiatric conditions. There are large numbers of descriptions of children with autism who do not eat or only eat very few different things, and there is plenty of clinical experience of eating disorders in girls with Asperger's syndrome. Besides, anorexia is often described as the result of a

---

[*]   Cooper *et al.* 2007; Turner 1989.

[**]   See for example recommendations for the use of medication from the University of Birmingham: Deb, Clarke and Unwin (2006).

childhood with great demands, not least the person's own demands to achieve. Consequently, we may consider eating disorders as the result of stress over a long period of time.

ANXIETY STATES

Anxiety states have been mentioned in relation to neuropsychiatric disorders ever since they were first described. But not all anxiety states can be considered long-term signs of chaos; some may be warning signs and some, like phobia of spiders, are more common in the general population.

In our work, when we are concerned about anxiety it is often because of social phobia or fear of leaving the home.[*]

> **Brigitte** is 53 years old. She went to a rural school and managed her way through elementary school, but was described as a socially isolated child. At the age of 15 she met a psychiatrist who described her as anxiety-ridden. She was early retired when she was 19. Brigitte never moved away from home, but lived with her parents until she was 49 years old when she was remitted to hospital for a cyst on her ovary. The cyst contained 50 litres of water, which made her look very pregnant, as a doctor put it. Brigitte is a small woman who normally weighs less than 45 kg.
>
> It turned out that Brigitte rarely left home and that she did not like people she did not know. She had kept indoors for several years and spent her time sewing her own clothes and doing other handicrafts. The local authorities were worried that she had become strange from not moving from home, but the psychological assessment that was carried out showed that she had Asperger's syndrome. Therefore she was moved to a group home.
>
> Brigitte does not like to leave the group home, and prefers to stay in her room. She is frightened when people look at her and she is afraid of what will happen if you walk around in town.

---

[*]   Kanner (1943), who first described autism, described anxiety as common in autism, just as at an early stage it had been in ADHD. In later years Muris *et al.* (1998) have shown that fully 84 per cent of all children within the autism spectrum met the diagnostic criteria for an anxiety state.

Her life is planned for her preferred activities and is very limited by her anxiety.

Brigitte is extremely disabled by her social difficulties, but even more by her anxiety. The staff and carers around her must focus on the anxiety, both in her treatment and by working with basic stress factors, if her quality of life is to be increased.

The long-lasting signs of chaos we have just gone through can sometimes be misinterpreted as problems in themselves. We do not think that they are. We think that they are the result of too high stress over time, which moves the focus of treatment from treating the person with the problem to adjusting the environment according to his or her needs. Unfortunately this does not mean that we always are able to remove the psychoses or anxiety states, but we can at least make sure that the quality of life is as high as possible.

Protective or calming factors

Luckily enough there are factors that help minimize the risk of experiences of chaos. They are called different things in literature. We call them protective factors whereas researcher Antonovsky has called them salutogenesis or health factors. He argues that these factors protect against stress and risk factors of mental illness.[*]

Some of these are the staff's or parents' responsibility and some are coping-oriented and have to do with the service-user's resources and strategies.

Personal protective factors

Personal protective factors include:

- everyday strategies
- self-knowledge
- independence
- optimism and humour

---

[*] Antonovsky 1991.

- being good at something
- emergency exits
- optional identity
- trust.

EVERYDAY STRATEGIES

Good everyday strategies can all be very different. Toby is a good example:

Toby is a 12-year old with a developmental age of 18 months and is very sensitive to other people's emotions. If someone smiles, he hits out, if someone cries, he hits out and if someone is clearly stressed, he hits out. He is therefore given all his tutoring alone, and the teachers relieve each other every second hour to be able to shield off. One day he develops a strategy to stay calm despite other people's affect. He discovers that if he breathes slowly and deeply when other people are restless he is able to keep his calm. He can consequently be moved back to the classroom with the other pupils.

Other everyday strategies are much more complex:

Avery is 25 years old and has Asperger's syndrome. He has participated in a course and encountered our stress model when it was under development. He was the one who said that there are two kinds of stress factors – those that are there every day and those that are there only at times – which led to the development of the basic and situational stress factors.

Avery tries to make his life come together and he soon identified his warning signs: he does not take out the rubbish when he is stressed (he once had 36 rubbish bags in the sitting room, which was a stress in itself) and he does not manage his commitments.

Every day he grades how he has slept and sets that out in an Excel version of the model so he is aware of his stress level. Then he says that a situational stress factor like for example a party takes three days to fade out. If he has an exam on the Monday he therefore must stay in all weekend. Once he explained to his grandmother who is 80 years old that he could not come at her birthday because of an exam two days later and mailed her the model so she would understand. Other times he can go away and do big things, as there is nothing else happening for a while. Among other things he has gone to the US by himself to attend a conference, but then he had made room for a month's holiday at home afterwards.

These two men's everyday strategies help them manage situations that might otherwise be disabling. They have come up with the strategies themselves and use them because they help. That is coping on a quite high level.

SELF-KNOWLEDGE

Self-knowledge is not always that simple. Some people go to psychotherapy for years to achieve self-knowledge without having any actual psychiatric problems. The self-knowledge of our service-users varies widely, but it is not always about having the best self-knowledge for it to be a protective factor. What is most important is that what you know about yourself and your reactions is of use in daily life.

Both Toby and Avery have self-knowledge enough to be able to use it to do better in daily life. Material like the CAT-kit (a cognitive-affective tool, see cat-kit.com) can be of help to increase the service-user's knowledge of him- or herself, as it may be really good to learn how the body works and how anxiety is felt in the body.

Some people develop self-knowledge focusing on stress levels or the need to be alone, and others the ability to seek help when needed.

INDEPENDENCE

Independence has already been described by Antonovsky as a protective factor. He thought that great enough freedom as a child brings an independence that is important to our resistance to stress. How this can be transferred to our focus group we are not completely sure, but in ADHD and Asperger's syndrome it should work. Perhaps it is the word *enough* that should be adjusted to the group.

OPTIMISM AND HUMOUR

Optimism can help people handle strains in daily life. Optimistic people do better in difficult situations than pessimists. Humour has also proved a way to protect oneself from stress. If you can laugh at yourself and your failures you do better.[*]

BEING GOOD AT SOMETHING

Being good at something is another protective factor. It doesn't matter what you are good at as long as you think it is important yourself.

> **Tyrah** has Asperger's syndrome. She is in seventh grade and thinks it is much easier to understand cats than people. Tyrah knows a lot about cats. When she started in her class in a regular elementary school she told her classmates that she knew all about cats and that if they had any questions they were welcome to ask her.
>
> Tyrah is quite isolated socially. She has one good friend who however is not in her class, so in school hours she is by herself a lot. After four years, Tyrah does not know the names of more than a few people in her class. She does however feel accepted and socially secure and the reason she offers is: 'I'm the one who knows all about cats. Twice one of my classmates has asked for my help, so I'm needed.'

Another small reflection is that if you are doing something you are good at, it often brings joy, and being happy is an important protective factor. In that way a special interest can be a protective factor and a way to deal with your stress.

---

[*]   Cernerud 2004.

EMERGENCY EXITS

Emergency exits giving a possibility for withdrawal may ensure being able to take part in contexts you never would otherwise. You get a possibility to shield off the surrounding world. The reader perhaps remembers the story about Leo and the soap bubbles? Here is another:

> **Tyrah,** whom we just met, had from the start a need to shield off at regular intervals at school. Therefore they arranged a seat in a double closet for her. There they put blankets, a pillow and a pile of Spiderman comics, and they put up a reading lamp. When Tyrah had a need for withdrawing she went into the closet and stayed there for a while. To begin with that was on average an hour a day, while by fifth grade she was down to 20 minutes.

Some people have solved their need for an emergency exit by running off when it gets hard. It does not have to go this far; you can sometimes strike a deal about where the service-user should go if he or she needs to be on his or her own. It is better for a pupil to go down to the ball court for half an hour than to run home through traffic when upset.

Another emergency exit is for there to be someone to call for help.

> **Mehmet** is 19 years old today. He has ADHD. When he went to school he had struck a deal with his father that no matter what happened he could always call him and then he would come pick him up. He could however only call if it was of absolute necessity.
>
> When Mehmet was in second grade he called once, and the next time was when he was in seventh grade. Both times his father came and picked him up. Every morning they had this stereotypical conversation:
>
> Mehmet: 'What should I do if it gets all too hard and absolutely, absolutely necessary?'
>
> Father: 'Then you just call me.'
>
> Mehmet: 'And what do you do then, Father?'
>
> Father: 'Then I start up the Toyota and come to get you!'

When Mehmet was in secondary school he was going to Spain to visit a Spanish secondary class. They were going to live with the Spanish families. This is a situation that may be very hard for Mehmet. He did not know the language, he did not know anybody, and he was going to stay with the Spanish family by himself. He asked his father: 'If it is absolutely, absolutely necessary, can I call you from Spain, even though it's far away?' The father replied: 'Yes, I just start up the Toyota and come to get you.'

When the plane was about to land Mehmet realized that he was about to land on a relatively small island. It was not just Spain, it was on one of the Canary Islands. He panicked and well out of the plane he immediately called his father: 'Father, I'm on Tenerife, and there are no roads here, it's an island. What should I do if it gets too hard? You can't drive here.'

Mehmet's father is a wise man, so he said: 'If it's absolutely, absolutely necessary you just call me. Then I go out and start up the Toyota and then I come to pick you up.'

Mehmet never had the need to call his father so they did not have to find out if the Toyota could drive on water. Mehmet's father said exactly the right words to calm Mehmet.

The value of this emergency exit is not that Mehmet can get out when it gets too hard, but that Mehmet can stay in the difficult situation because he knows that there is a legitimate way out. Exactly the same thing is true for Tyrah with her Spiderman comics in the closet, Charlie who hides in the TV cabinet and Leo and his soap bubbles. They endure daily life because there is a legitimate way to get out if it gets too hard.

Sometimes I meet staff or parents who argue that you cannot use emergency exits because the service-users will only try to get out all the time and avoid everything that is hard. I do not think so. I believe that people who can behave, will, and I think that our service-users want to develop and try new and difficult things. But sometimes they have been subjected to too much and are therefore reluctant to rise to demands and challenges. Then we must adjust the demands so the service-user dares be challenged again. This usually works. We cannot lose faith in the service-user and then pressure him or her through experiences he or she cannot handle; that is assault.

> **Marco** is 15 years old and has Asperger's syndrome. He has quit school and now stays at home playing World of Warcraft instead. He does not shower and does not clean his room. After a while he is admitted to a child psychiatry clinic, but is discharged again as they think there is nothing they can do.
>
> His parents get guidance, and the consultant maintains that we must give him time and surplus by giving him positive feedback and faith that it will pass. His father, however, finds this very hard; he keeps returning to it being about laziness – Marco wants to sit at home and play rather than go to school, so the pressure on him should be increased.
>
> The consultant's argument is simple and hard to resist: if an ordinary teenage boy is given the choice between sitting at home in front of the computer smelling like a pile of rubbish and going to school with his friends with the chance to discover the opposite sex, which would he choose? Marco sits where he sits because it is necessary in his life right now.

OPTIONAL IDENTITY

Optional identity is a way of coming to terms with existential issues in the teens and for people with social shortcomings for the rest of their lives. In some groups it is a common coping strategy.

> **Tania** is 17 years old. She has Asperger's syndrome. One day when she was 16 years old she told her mother that she was going to be a goth. Her mother did not know what that was, so Tania told her that was youths who wore black clothes, liked hard rock music and sometimes cut their arms. Tania said that she did not think that she would cut her arms, but she wanted the rest. She began collecting black clothes, shoes, makeup and jewellery in goth style, and suddenly one Wednesday morning she went to school as a fully-fledged goth. The reactions from her classmates were mixed, but Tania countered by saying: 'You can be as you wish, right?'

In the coming months Tania made more friends than she had ever had before. They were young people she met in town who made contact with her because she wore similar clothes. Tania says: 'The best thing I've done was to be a goth. I know what to think, I know what words to use and what to do to fit in.' It should be noted than no one is as thorough in his or her style as Tania.

When Tania is meeting her grandmother she does not wear goth clothes. Then she is the old Tania who is a bit awkward and does not really know how to fit in.

Tania puts on a goth persona and then it is easier to manage socially. She becomes the person she wishes to be, and it also means that she gets a clear group belonging, which is another protective factor.

Bruce is 44 years old. Ever since he was little he has had problems managing socially. He was quite a nerd as a boy; he liked toy trains and electronics. After secondary school he studied to become an engineer and started working at a company making phone systems. Now he is head of production at a similar company.

We got in contact with Bruce because his son got an Asperger diagnosis, and Bruce told us that he thought it was hard to know how to be a good father to his son. He says: 'I'm good at putting on identities. If I look for a new job I read the ad to see what kind of co-worker they want. Then I put that co-worker on and go there. I've done several personality tests in my job-seeking with very different results. In my job I put on the co-worker they want and that works really well. At home I put on the husband and the father to my daughter, but I don't know what to do in relation to my son. There is no one to copy and he plays at parts of me that makes it difficult.'

Bruce probably has Asperger's syndrome, but as his strategies work well he is not given a diagnosis. He does well in daily life. His strategy is, like Tania's, to assume another persona. Bruce says that his wife often asks him who he is deep inside, but he says: 'There is no one. I am the people I assume and that is good.' And it is good, he has done well in life, he has reached a quite high position in working life, has been married for 18 years and has two children, and he makes his finances come together.

Identity as a coping strategy has a tendency to be very thorough. No one is as goth as Tania, and the person who is the most hip hop perhaps also has the need to put on that identity. Most people who build their identity take a little from different groups and find their own balance. Those with Asperger's syndrome probably will not find the balance but take on the identity completely.

This does however not mean that you have put on an identity forever. Bruce says that there is no core personality in him and therefore he can change identity just like that.

> **Mick** is 19 years old and has Asperger's syndrome. He became a Nazi when he was 16 years old and started shaving his head and wearing folded jeans and black boots. His opinions worked well with his black-and-white basic views and inability to see nuances. The first consequence of his choice of identity was that he was thrown out of a club for young people with Asperger's syndrome he was a member of.
>
> In secondary school he often had to defend his opinions and he gladly did so, which did not render him popular. After about half a year as a Nazi he got beaten up in town three Saturday nights in a row. So he decided to quit being a Nazi. He became a communist instead. He himself says: 'It's easier, then you don't get beaten up and you can be friends with immigrants.'

TRUST

Trust in people in the world around you is another protective factor. You cannot always influence your level of trust yourself, so part of the responsibility lies in the people around you.

If you are with someone you trust, you manage situations you otherwise would not. Previously we used the delivery ward as an example; it is important that you have someone you trust with you at the delivery ward when you are about to give birth, otherwise it will be a much harder task. In the same way children look for their parents when they have nightmares or something bad happens. Therefore our methods must be based on building trust, then the service-user gets more surplus and manages daily life better.

External protective factors

Other protective factors are more up to the people around the person. Some of these are very reminiscent of pedagogy. This is perhaps not that strange; good pedagogy limits the stress and adjusts demands. Protective factors around the person may be about:

- structure
- common understanding
- adjustment of demands
- possibility of withdrawal
- relationship networking
- social support.

STRUCTURE

Structure is a standard educational and care tool. In the neuro-psychiatric field it is the starting point for good pedagogy, and has been so in the Nordic countries since we began with special education. Structure has been truly in focus since the introduction of TEACCH in the autism field, but the tool was also a great part of some of the psychodynamic methods developed in the 1970s and 1980s for children with challenging behaviour.

I have said it before in this book, but it stands to be repeated. Structure is for the service-user, not the staff, which means that the structure should be based on the service-user's needs and not be a strict daily programme meant to work for everybody. Besides, different service-users need different kinds of and degrees of structure. Structure is there to compensate for a lack of understanding of contexts, not because the service-users are dependent on it. This means that the structure should be based on predictability and therefore be clear to the service-user. The structure cannot be a way for the service-user to accept the staff's authority.

When a structure is good it brings clarity and predictability, which means that the service-user can relax and be secure. Nothing surprising will happen, which many service-users benefit from. In most people's daily life nothing surprising happens either. We can predict what will happen most of the time, and if something unpredicted happens we still understand why most of the time. If you have problems understanding contexts you can neither predict particularly well, nor understand why it happened if something unpredicted happens. Unpredicted events therefore not only increase the insecurity in the situation itself, but often bring an increased general insecurity for a long time ahead. If an unpredicted event can happen, perhaps anything can happen, and that means you can never know when earth will go under or when a dragon will eat you.

COMMON UNDERSTANDING

A common understanding of the problems from the world around the person means fewer conflicts. Neighbours don't say 'How can you let him do so?' to parents of children with challenging behaviour if they know that the child is not like other children and that he is doing his best. This brings a greater security to the parents and a greater predictability to the child. In the same way, all teachers in a school should have the same attitude to a child with challenging behaviour.

The reader perhaps remembers Leo with the soap bubbles. If the other teachers of the school were not aware of the method, they would scold Leo when standing in the corridor blowing soap bubbles. That would probably have meant some dirty words from Leo and quite a few conflicts.

In chapter one, we took a look at the tendency to blame someone else when you do not have the tools necessary. When different groups of staff, staff and relatives or staff and management start to blame other people, it not only ruins the cooperation, it often fixes the service-user into a behaviour no one can affect. You have to take on responsibility to be able to exert influence.

Therefore it is incredibly important that all parties aim to create a common understanding of the problems.

ADJUSTMENT OF DEMANDS

I have brought this up previously. It is, however, a truly important protective factor that we in the world around the person can take responsibility for.

POSSIBILITY OF WITHDRAWAL

The possibility for withdrawal by the service-user is related to the emergency exits just discussed. The reason for bringing this up again is that the people around the service-user sometimes have to create the possibility for the service-user to withdraw by making an agreement about where the service-user can go, by building shacks they can be in or by adjusting a closet, as we did for Tyrah.

RELATIONSHIP NETWORKS

Good relationship networks have for many years been described as an important factor to compensate for a poor social environment. If children have good friends and some good relationships with adults, even if they grow up in poor social circumstances they still manage fairly well.

For some children with challenging behaviour, non-educational staff are very important. These can be the caretaker at the school or a grandfather, people who do not make the same demands on them in daily life as parents and educational staff do. That is one of the reasons why we like it when institutions invite the caretaker or the canteen staff to courses in managing challenging behaviour. Their part is not to pressure or take responsibility for the children's development, but they can improve their general wellbeing, which on the whole is what we think is the most important thing.

For service-users with a great need of assistance, it may be enough to say hello to a neighbour to feel that they have some relationship, whereas service-users with a high level of function demand true friendships. This brings us to the last, but not the least important example of a protective factor.[*]

SOCIAL SUPPORT

It has been shown in research that social support can reduce stress hormones in the body. Likewise it has been shown that the delay in healing of wounds that has been seen as a warning sign in stress disappears if you get social assistance. You can as a member of staff

---

[*]   Antonovsky 1991; Cederblad 1996.

or parent with quite small means talk to the service-user about what is hard and how she or he is feeling.*

The stress model can be used as a mapping tool for behaviour or symptoms, but it can also be used as the basis for treatment. We have worked with young people who have been able to relate to the model themselves and even used it as a navigation tool in daily life. I have had some feedback from schools, among others a girl in a school for children with ADHD or Asperger's syndrome in the outskirts of Copenhagen. She described to her teachers that she was under quite high stress right now and therefore asked to be relieved from homework over the weekend. Among other things, her grandmother had passed away. The teachers said: 'It was obvious that she had gone to a self-understanding course with Trine Uhrskov and we decided to reduce the demands regarding homework for a while. That she can express her lack of surplus we must consider something positive.'

Working with the model it may be relevant to qualify the stress factors so we do not remove only the fun experiences.

> **Lin** is 16 years old and has quit school. When she was eight years old she got an ADHD diagnosis that in her early teens was changed to an Asperger's diagnosis. Last year she developed psychotic symptoms, which brought a palpable reduction of quality of life.
>
> Lin has mapped her stress with the assistance of a carer and has reached the conclusion that the most important stress factors are: the demand to go to school, taking care of her horse, difficulties understanding the world around her, social difficulties, and a constant unpredictability. The most important situational stress factors are: when mother and father have friends coming over (which happens nearly every weekend), social situations in the stables, some food situations, and when she does not know what to do.
>
> In cooperation with her parents it was therefore decided that Lin should be relieved of the demand to go to school (she is in ninth grade and school is nearly over anyway), but that she

---

* Detillion *et al.* 2004; Ditzen *et al.* 2008.

should continue with riding school and taking care of her horse, and that the carer will be there for her to facilitate social situations. They create a good daily structure that accommodates activities like drawing and sculpting (Lin is really good at drawing and sculpting horses). Her parents go to visit their friends instead of having them over.

In this way, Lin kept those activities that meant quality of life (those that had to do with horses) but was relieved of the activities that were only stress. To skip school and keep riding school perhaps is not what you would usually have chosen, but in this case it was relevant to protect Lin from her psychotic symptoms.

Summary

Stress is a major cause of challenging behaviour. Stress can be viewed as pressure from the surroundings, but can also be viewed in relation to the cognitive deficits found in intellectual disability and neuropsychiatric deficits. The chapter introduces a model for mapping out stress factors and challenging behaviour in order to change the surroundings and its demands, thereby reducing challenging behaviour.

The model stresses the importance of separating basic and situational stress factors in order to make changes in the everyday framework that will make a difference in the long run. It also separates stress-related warning signs from signs of chaos in order to let staff and parents know when an intervention may be needed. Finally, protective strategies are introduced, strategies for staff, parents or the service-users themselves that help the service-user endure stress.

Chapter 5

· · · · · · ·

When Conflict Happens: Keeping It Calm

So far we have looked at everything that might go wrong and lead to conflicts, and how you as a member of staff can avoid that outcome. Unfortunately, this means we do not always succeed. There will be conflicts even if you have read this book. Furthermore, conflicts arise for reasons we cannot control. This may be conflicts between service-users or in situations where the service-user meets people who do not have an educational or care responsibility, for example in the tube, in the store or on a walk. This chapter will hopefully give you tools to handle conflicts and violent behaviour when they actually happen.

Different methods for managing violent behaviour have been used throughout time, which we have already discussed. We have seen different kinds of restraints, from control holds to methods based on self-defence, where you get the service-user where you want by causing him or her pain, for example by armlocks. We ought not forget the belts in psychiatric wards either, where there is a long tradition of mechanical restraint.

Our point of departure must be to create optimal conditions for the service-user to regain self-control as quickly as possible. As staff or parents we should not increase the level of conflict, but have methods to reduce it and also reduce the service-user's stress in the situation. We began to deal with this in chapter three 'Adjustment of Demands', but now we will take the discussion a step further. First we must take a look at some fundamental affect theory.

Theories of affect and emotion contagion

Charles Darwin discovered in the 1860s that some basic emotions of humans and certain animals brought similar facial expressions. He also explored whether emotional expressions were the same all over the world and came to the conclusion that a fairly small number of emotions were more basic than others and consequently should be considered hereditary, species-specific, biological programmes. Darwin found six basal emotions and affects. Since then researchers and theorists like William James, Carl Lange, Silvan Tomkins, Paul Ekman, John Bowlby, Donald Nathanson and not least Daniel Stern have developed affect theory so today we believe that man has at least nine different basal affects:

- interest
- distress
- anger
- disgust
- weariness
- surprise
- joy
- fear
- shame.

These affects are distinguished by manifest expressions that can be considered both biological and psychological, which means that they can be felt as the result of an experience or a memory, but also that they can be set in motion by affecting the chemistry of the brain, for example through drugs or medication. Most of them are in effect from birth, but joy, fear and shame are developed in the first year of life.[*]

The different affects can be felt more or less forcefully. You can be a little distressed or very distressed, you can be a little surprised or

---

[*]   Bowlby 1973, 1980, 1999 (1969); Darwin 1998 (1867); Ekman 2003; James 1884; Lange 1887; Nathanson 1992; Stern 1985, 2004; Tomkins 1962, 1963, 1991.

very surprised and joy, anger and interest can be graded in different ways. All affects can be too much for a small child who has not learnt to shield off yet. You can be so happy you bite your mother or lose self-control in another way. Strong affect is in this way not only a situational stress factor, but triggers quite a lot of challenging behaviour. Nobody fights when calm, but because you are upset.

In relation to challenging behaviour, it is not the affects themselves that are interesting, but how forcefully they are felt and how they are passed on.

> **Elliot** is four weeks old. He is a calm baby and the family's first child. His mother, Erica, likes to go for coffee with a group of mothers. They are five mothers who often meet up.
>
> One day when they are at an espresso café having lattes Elliot is hungry. He is lying in his carrier, just like the other children. When you are four weeks old it is not certain that you know you are hungry, but you know that you get an unpleasant feeling in your body and that triggers an affect: you are distressed and begin to cry.
>
> And now the magical thing happens: when Elliot starts crying everything is fine for a few seconds, then one of the other babies starts crying and another one and another one even though they are not hungry. It is not the hunger that is infectious, but the sadness.

Emotion contagion is obvious in infants. Daniel Stern has also described how we adults use emotion contagion in our contact with children. If the child is happy about accomplishing something, so are we; and the two of us experience the shared happiness, which deepens it. If the child is sad, we talk with a slightly subdued tone of voice. When we have made contact we shift the child's affect to a happier one by changing our tone of voice. Stern calls this affective *attunement* and gives it an important place in his theory on psychological development.[*]

In adults, emotion contagion is not as obvious. We have learnt to shield off in order not to be too influenced by other people, and

---

[*]   Stern 1985.

we have learnt to shield off other people from our own affects. These skills we use to different degrees in different relationships and situations. With a loved one we trust we do not shield off as much, but use emotion contagion to interact with each other in what Stern calls *intersubjectivity*, which can, for example, be seen in how we move towards each other when cooperating, and in the dance of coordinated movements that arises when two lovers sit opposite each other. Among other things, we use touch and eye contact to enhance emotion contagion when we want to reach a feeling of kinship and intersubjectivity.[*]

When we are under stress, however, it is harder to shield off affectively and we are more sensitive to other people's affect, for example other people find us easier to read emotionally because we do not shield off our affect as much as we normally do.

One of the mechanisms behind emotion contagion is probably what is called mirror neurons, brain cells that are in those areas of the brain that control motor activity. These cells react to other people's actions. If someone smiles, the smile is mirrored in our mirror neurons, which get a parallel activity pattern to what we have when we smile ourselves. Therefore it is not surprising that it is hard not to smile back.

One of the most effective ways to limit challenging behaviour in the form of acting-out behaviour and self-harm is first to make sure that you do not increase the service-user's affect and second to use emotion contagion to reduce the service-user's affect.

There are some interesting projects of research where this has been looked at. In one study they found that if the staff are under stress there are more incidents,[**] and in another that the social climate in an institution influences the behaviour of the service-users.[***]

Most of the situational mental load factors that were described in chapter four increase the level of affect:

- *Explicit demands* are sometimes made, and we expect service-users to be able to do what we ask of them. This may be to

---

[*]   Stern 2004.

[**]   Rose and Rose 2005.

[***] Langdon, Swift and Budd 2006.

eat properly, to return something a service-user has taken in a store, to be quiet or to clean his or her room. If for whatever reason they cannot live up to the demands, they will react with anxiety and insecurity, which means an increase in intensity of affect.

- *Conflicts* are characterized by the increase of level of affect in two people. I have never been in conflict with a calm person and never myself been calm in a conflict. Either I react affectively to something, which starts the conflict, or I react to another person's affect and enter the conflict.

- *Scolding* often triggers an affective reaction. This is easy to see if you turn to yourself and imagine how upset you would be if your boss were to tell you off.

- *Not understanding* gives rise to frustration, an increase in intensity of affect.

- *Sudden noises* bring surprise or an experience of shock, which is a fundamental affect.

- *Sudden changes* are extremely frustrating to people with reduced flexibility.

All these situations are characterized by frustration. Frustration is an increase in intensity of affect, often of anxiety. We can therefore accept that people with challenging behaviour, regardless of diagnosis, have in common a reduced ability to regulate affect. The small child loses control if he or she is hungry. Most adults do not. Our ability to regulate affect increases with age, but my experience is that this development does not fully function in the service-users I meet. They may be young people with Asperger's syndrome who easily break into tears, or a boy with ADHD who bangs his fist into a wall when something does not go his way.

However, challenging behaviour can be triggered by other affects as well:

Yunus is 11 years old and has ADHD. He is sitting in the canteen in school eating rice with sausage casserole. Yunus has some motor difficulties and therefore is messy with his food. He finds it difficult to eat in a proper way and to keep the food on the plate. When he has finished, he takes his plate and goes towards the washing-up. A canteen staff member stops him and tells him off: 'See how you've soiled the whole table. Go and get a cloth and clean up after yourself!' Yunus reacts by scolding back: 'You should serve food that can be eaten, bitch. The rice can't be put on the fork without spilling.'

Pedro is 21 years old and has autism. His father wants Pedro to have many good experiences. One day they go to see a football game between Manchester United and Liverpool. They are in the Liverpool stand with the supporters. When Liverpool score the first goal the crowd in the stand is ecstatic. Pedro reacts to the joy by knocking out six people around him, including his father.

Yunus' problem in this situation is not that he spills, but that he immediately reacts to the canteen lady's anger, without knowing why he is mad. Pedro immediately reacts to the infectious joy but cannot regulate his affect and so experiences chaos. The affective pressure in a football stand is incredibly high and more than Pedro can handle.

The two boys have problems separating their own and other people's affects. This is a difficulty experienced by most people with neuropsychiatric disorders, and it is also common in people with intellectual disabilities. Why that is the case we do not know, nor what the consequences for the personality development will be in the long run.

Personally, I believe that this is part of the development of empathy: we start out with a good ability of emotion contagion. Somewhere between 18 months and four years of age most people develop the ability to separate their own and other people's affect, which means, for example, that you can begin to comfort other people. Some time later these skills are slowly beginning to be used in the development of what is called theory of mind or mentalization ability, which means that you are able to predict other people's states of mind, thoughts and intentions.[*]

We use our mentalization ability every day and in many situations. If we meet someone on a narrow pavement, we must estimate in which direction the other person will go to be able to place ourselves correctly. If we meet a group of rowdy young men with shaved heads and boots on a dark night, we are likely to cross the road. In the beginning of a love relationship one of the two must take the right initiative, but mentalization ability is required to take the initiative at the right time.

Thus, the foundation of intersubjectivity is that we are able to put ourselves in another person's shoes and adjust our behaviour accordingly so we reach what Daniel Stern calls the *dance of intersubjectivity*.[**]

Autism is often described as having difficulties with the mentalization ability. I am not thoroughly convinced about that. My experience is that some people with Asperger's syndrome, which is a disorder in the autism spectrum, are able to estimate other people's states of mind, thoughts and intentions. The development is however slow, often many years into adult life, and they rarely reach the level of ordinary people. Furthermore, it is a requirement that you know when a situation requires this kind of estimation. A good friend of mine who is in his sixties and has Asperger's syndrome performs normally on a test of mentalization ability. However, he is not always logged on; for example in the spring of 2008 he was hit in what could be called an autism collision. He was standing waiting for a green signal at a pedestrian crossing. When it turned to green for him he walked straight out into the road despite the fact that a car was coming at full speed. He did not mentalize the speed of the driver and his chances of stopping in time. It may be the case that the empathy disorder in autism is not founded on actual problems with mentalization ability, but on difficulties separating your own and other people's affect, which must be the foundation of the mentalization ability.

---

[*] Frith 2003.

[**] Stern 2004.

In my work with guidance of managing challenging behaviour, I find that an important factor in daily life is that people with autism or other neuropsychiatric disorders have great difficulties separating their own affect from that of other people. In Yunus this can be seen when he scolds the person scolding him, and it can also be seen in the anxiety that is spread if one member of staff at a group home or in a special school class is late and is stressed.

This means that service-users' reactions to our affects are not always what we expect them to be. If I am angry with my children at home, I expect them to know that I am angry and use that knowledge when planning their behaviour. If I am angry at a service-user, something completely different happens. First, the service-user may get angry back. Many people who work in the field of special education describe how service-users scold back if you tell them off.

Or second the service-user may begin to laugh. A way to process heightened affect is to laugh. I experienced this once myself in a highly embarrassing way when my partner and I were at the movies. We saw Benigni's movie *Life Is Beautiful*. The movie is about a father and his son's experiences in a German concentration camp in the Second World War. At the end of the movie foreign troops are taking over the camp. The father hides his son in a locker so he will not get into danger in the reigning chaos. A camp guard finds the father, pushes him behind a wall and shoots him. That, I was not prepared for. I always expect the hero to survive. I did not know how to deal with the feeling triggered by this and laughed out loud. I was definitely the only one in the theatre who laughed. When you laugh you release affect. In a joke an expectation is built up that is never set free; the answer is always unexpected and then you laugh. If the service-user wants to get rid of an unexpected affect, he or she can always laugh it away. But if he or she does so, it is not always certain that we understand what is happening. We may misjudge the motives of the service-user and think that he or she is laughing at us.

Or third, the service-user may experience chaos. If he or she cannot shield off the experienced affect and the affect is too powerful in its intensity, he or she loses self-control. Then he or she may begin to hit out and scream or be overwhelmed with anxiety.

The research on strong feelings in a person's surroundings that I mentioned in chapter four can be readily understood in the context of this difficulty separating our own and other people's affect. If you experience different, strong feelings all the time but do not know why, it is not surprising that behaviour is affected. This must create insecurity in daily life.

Another aspect of this is the inability to shield off other people from your own affect if you cannot relate to the difference between your own and other people's affect. The first time I entered a room with ten adults with intellectual disabilities and autism I was overwhelmed by the affect in the room. It was like a great affective wall. Newly employed staff often talk about being awfully tired the first week they work with this type of service-user. The reason is that we usually shield off other people from our affect, for example we control our emotional expressions by turning away if we are affected emotionally or by regulating our eye contact. People with special needs do not.

Small children do not shield off other people from their affect either, but use it to communicate with the world around them. This is crucial for the children's survival as long as they must have help with both food and body functions and before they have developed other ways of communication. When they begin to develop a language, the communication is moved to the language and the need of affective communication is reduced. At the same time they begin to develop the ability to separate their own and other people's affect and consequently also to shield us off.

The greatest difference between the affect radiation from a baby and that from an adult with an intellectual disability is the size of the sender. A small transmitter transmits a small signal and a big one transmits a big signal. There is a difference in size between a baby and an adult and the affect's physical expression, and the level of emotion contagion increases accordingly, because we probably find it much harder to shield off the signal from an adult. Moreover, it probably also matters that we expect an affective signal from the baby as that is the baby's foremost way of communication, whereas we do not expect a strong affective signal from an adult. The adult's strong emotion contagion makes us uncertain of what might happen; strong affective signals normally means unpredictability.

Emotion contagion and the lack of ability to separate his or her affects from those of other people means that the service-user is sensitive to our affects. In situations of crises this means that our affective reactions have a great impact on the service-user's behaviour. If we are stressed by the service-user's behaviour, our stress will mean that he or she is further stressed, which strengthens his or her behaviour. If we react affectively, perhaps angrily, in a demand situation there is a risk that the increase of affect because of the demand is further strengthened by our affective reaction, which increases the risk of challenging behaviour. This can be illustrated by an image of how the intensity of affect is increased (Figure 5.1).

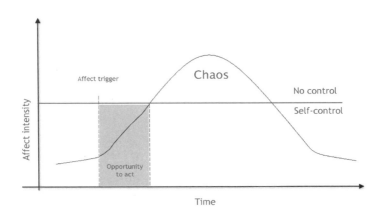

Figure 5.1 How a service-user's intensity of affect is heightened by affective reactions

The stars are our reactions. An affect is triggered in the service-user by an incident that may be a demand, a change or something else. The service-user will in most cases try to reduce his or her affect quickly to keep self-control, perhaps by refusing, biting their hand or by walking away from the situation. If you as a member of staff or a parent react emotionally, are afraid or angry, the service-user's affect will increase and the possibility of him or her retaining self-control is reduced. The risk of chaotic behaviour is increased.

The low-arousal approach

We must meet the service-user in a way that does not increase his or her affect, just like we must control ourselves so we do not react with strong affects. This can be done in various different ways, which I discuss in more detail below:

- react in a controlled way
- avoid eye contact
- avoid touch
- respect personal space
- avoid emphasizing yourself
- sit down
- talk calmly
- give in
- change the staff
- use the 'snooker trick'
- wait.

Reacting in a controlled way

We have previously discussed the expression *expressed emotion* where I argued that service-users feel better if we keep our emotions in check. The reason for expressed emotion being harmful is perhaps that service-users experience the same feeling as we do, but they have no idea why. It is like being on an emotional roller-coaster; you have no idea what will happen after the next turn.

My own strategy is to stay calm. It is not that difficult for me; I am calmed by controlling my breathing. A colleague of mine finds it very difficult, but has another strategy: he can stay calm on the outside by controlling his breathing, his movements and keeping his distance, despite being anxious on the inside. Both strategies work.

I often say that we should be a little more relaxed in our ways and avoid dramatic emotional expressions. Then the service-users are most at ease and we will not provoke any affective outbreaks.

Avoiding eye contact

We use eye contact for different reasons and in different situations. Daniel Stern once said that eye contact that is held for more than 20 seconds always ends in either sex or violence. What he means is that in situations where we either wish to seduce someone or wish to start a fight, we try to 'secure the emotion contagion' and make sure that the other person has the same affect as ourselves. We must agree on fighting or having sex, or it will not be right.

Therefore we can see how people avoid eye contact with an angry man in a dark street. We do not want any contact with him and perhaps be pulled into an escalation of affect. We do not want to agree with him on a fight. My son Matthias has experimented with this. He has checked what happens if you suddenly begin to seek eye contact with the person next to you on the bus. He says that only a few moments pass before they get up and find another seat. We do not want that degree of intimacy with a stranger on the bus that a common affect brings.

We also use eye contact, however not for long, when we wish to dominate. Every time we say, 'Look at me when I'm talking to you' we try to make the other person understand how much we mean what we are saying. We rely on emotion contagion; by looking into our eyes the other person can read how angry or determined we are, but at the same time we rely on the other person to be able to recognize the source of the affect he or she experiences.

If the service-user does not know who has the original affect, he or she experiences a rise in affect intensity based on affect contagion when looking us in the eyes. The eye contact boosts the already existing emotion contagion with the risk of the service-user losing self-control.

Another aspect of eye contact as a risk of conflict is that eye contact always increases affect. This can be tested by looking another person in the eye from a distance of roughly half a metre for ten seconds. These ten seconds will feel incredibly long. In the ten seconds it will be hard not to laugh and it will be very hard to stay quiet, and we will really want to talk about the experience as soon as we look away again. We simply must process the experience.

Sometimes we do this in the same way as service-users often do – by laughing or by talking about it.

When we use eye contact in a situation of conflict with a service-user, the eye contact will not calm him or her down either. On the contrary, the eye contact will intensify the affect. The service-user, however, is rarely able to laugh the affect away or process it by talking. Instead the service-user's intensity of affect will increase and perhaps cause him or her to lose self-control and begin to react self-injuriously or act out.

Avoiding touch

When we grab a service-user, we rarely do so with loose, calm muscles, but with force and control. This means that the service-user feels the force and is infected. If you are to calm somebody with emotion contagion, you can do so by comforting with a loose arm on the shoulder, not by grabbing the arm with your hand.

In the neuropsychiatric field, it is not uncommon for a service-user to react forcefully on being touched, even to a calm hand on the shoulder. Many service-users experience the staff member's touch as a trigger of chaos experiences and respond with more acting-out behaviour, which makes the staff grab them harder, and so on.

My recommendation is not to use touch with a service-user at all in situations of conflict and only use a hand on the shoulder if you know him or her very well.

There are situations when you may be forced to grab a service-user. However, the criterion of lawful self-defence must be met. Consequently, there must be an immediate danger to life or health, either that of the service-user or of somebody else. Then we are no longer talking about a risk of conflict but about an ongoing violent conflict. In those cases you should however not grab a service-user unless you are trained in a method that focuses on the security of the service-user from a low-arousal point of origin. I recommend the British method Studio III.

Among other things, the Studio III method involves that you for a very short time, five to ten seconds, move with the service-user and using his or her movements to calm him or her. Then you let him or her go and he or she will experience soothing relief from your touch.

It is however of utmost importance that you learn and practise how to touch the service-user and what movements and holds should be avoided to ensure that the service-user is not harmed. If you do not have that practice, it is simply better, safer and more efficient not to touch the service-user at all. If other service-users' health is at risk, they can be led out instead of grabbing the conflicted service-user.

Another effect of emotion contagion is that if we grab a service-user in a room where there are other service-users, they will experience the same affects and intensity of affect as the person we take hold of. They have no possibility of shielding off and do not know who has the affect they feel. Our assault consequently is not an assault only on the person we grab, but also on all the others. In that way we traumatize all our service-users, which cannot be considered a part of our educational or care assignment.

If a service-user grabs my arm, there is a risk that I get tense, which means that the service-user gets even tenser. Often this is about the service-user wanting me to go with him or her somewhere. If I tense and put up some resistance, the service-user may get stronger and there is a risk that the situation develops negatively. If I instead relax the arm the service-user takes hold of, the service-user's hold is immediately softer and I can go with him or her and carefully get free on the way.

Respecting personal space

To be near other people can be a very nice experience. However, I do not like to be too near people I do not know well, just like it can be strenuous to be too near someone I know well if I am under stress or am upset.

I have a colleague who always stands a little too near me. He is a big man, half a head taller and perhaps 50 pounds heavier than me. I have realized that I am not able to understand what he is saying if it is only he and I talking. On the other hand, if another person joins the conversation there is no problem; then he keeps better distance. When it is only he and I the proximity stresses me and causes an increase in intensity of affect. This means that I must find strategies to reduce the intensity of affect, which I do by shielding off. This is however not good either for the conversation or the understanding.

When you are anxious you try, as has already been described in the section on self-control, to reduce the intensity of affect. A very good way is to create some distance. You could say that the necessary personal space increases with the intensity of affect. Many service-users take two steps away from us if they are anxious. That is a great strategy. The problem is that we as staff or parents often follow. We feel like we lose a little bit of control. To follow the person, however, does not mean more control. Instead it entails a great risk that the service-user is not able to keep his or her self-control and consequently experiences chaos. Therefore I want to introduce two simple ways of dealing with personal space:

- When the service-user steps away from you, take two steps backwards.
- Never stand face to face with a service-user in affect.

The first of these is perhaps the most effective tip in the whole book. The distance should at least be a couple of yards when the service-user is anxious.

For some years I have worked with a special school for pupils with Asperger's syndrome. When the school started they used physical restraints. The first time I met the staff the school had 25 pupils. We had an afternoon when among other things I introduced the principle of backing off. When I met the staff again the following year, a teacher told me that he had worked with a boy with severe challenging behaviour, who frequently had to be restrained. After having talked to me, the following day they had begun to walk backwards instead of forwards in a conflict and soon realized that that was very effective. They had not had to physically restrain that boy since. When I last met the staff of the school the school manager, who now leads a school of 75 pupils, said that it had been several years since they had used physical restraint at all.

By walking backwards instead of forwards you allow the service-user to keep his or her self-control. The distance helps the service-user shield off better, thereby reducing his or her intensity of affect. At the same time you create a better opportunity for shielding off the affect of the service-user yourself and in that way stay calm. We are not completely immune to emotion contagion just because we do not have neuropsychiatric problems or intellectual disabilities, and emotion contagion is harder to manage if we are stressed ourselves. To create a distance means that we can think more clearly and act in a more balanced way.

If there is a risk of the service-user attacking other service-users or any other people, this method naturally does not work. Then you must make everyone leave at once so the distance can be kept. If the problem is a conflict between two service-users, taking two steps backwards will not work either. In these cases diversion should be used, which we will discuss shortly.

In daily life we almost never stand completely in front of each other. Either there is a piece of furniture, for example a counter, between us or we stand slightly to one side of one another. It is only when we kiss or dance or when we want to challenge or dominate other people that we show the front of our body to each other. If you experiment with standing right in front of other people, you will soon discover that they quickly move so they are standing slightly to one side of you, or they are violent, or they kiss you. I recently held a course where I told the participants this on the first day. The next day one of the participants told me that she had stood right in front of her boyfriend when she got home. In a few seconds he had pushed her twice and when she stayed in place he had kissed her on the mouth. He was very confused and could not explain his reaction either to her or himself.

The reason for us sometimes placing ourselves in front of the service-user is the same as when we use eye contact: we try to dominate. There are several problems in doing so: we should not dominate, our aim is to make the service-users cooperate, and the dominance is based on affective methods that do not work in the field of special needs.

Standing in front of a service-user, even from a two-metre distance, means a doubled intensity of affect compared to standing slightly to the side looking slightly away from the service-user.

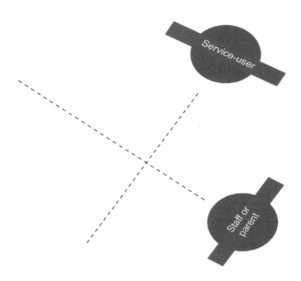

Figure 5.2 Creating calm by avoiding a face-to-face stance

By placing yourself as illustrated in Figure 5.2, you reduce the build-up of affect and create calm. Once again this is important for your own ability to stay calm; you shield off the service-user's affect and are consequently better at regulating your own affect.[*]

Avoiding emphasizing yourself

It may be difficult, particularly for men, to use this strategy. We are used to using our body as a dominating factor in daily life – tensing our muscles and broadening our shoulders. If somebody touches their upper arm, few men are able to avoid tensing their muscles. Sometimes you wonder how much trust we actually have in our masculinity having to act like that.

The problem with tensing in this way is that service-users often also tense. Emotion contagion is based on the fact that the muscles you use, I will use as well. We probably do so because the brain reads the other person's muscular tensions through so-called mirror

---

[*]   Hewett 1998; Whitaker 2001.

neuron processes, which give parallel muscular tensions in ourselves. To tense the whole upper body as you do when emphasizing yourself unfortunately means a lot of tension. In the service-user this will result in an increased intensity of affect and production of adrenaline, which increases the risk of conflict.

I worked at a group home for people with autism and violent behaviour outside Copenhagen. They hired a couple of former policemen as helpers. That was not a good idea. The thought was that they would be able to defend themselves if they were attacked, but it turned out that they were attacked much more often than the other employees. Apparently, they used a dominant body language to a higher degree than the other employees.

On the other hand, there is a group home in Jutland in Denmark where they have hired former UN soldiers for two service-users with highly challenging behaviour. Their experiences are truly positive. The difference is that the soldiers had over many years learnt to wait (that is done a lot in military service) and learnt to hide. The police officer should be visible, the soldier invisible. The two groups are trained in self-defence, but from two different perspectives.

Similarly, when the police tried not to use protection gear at demonstrations during the European Social Forum in Malmö, Sweden, in 2008, they reached the conclusion that this resulted in less rioting than on other occasions. To show strength to scare other people into avoiding challenging behaviour often has the opposite effect.[*]

A good example of us already knowing this deep down, but that we are not always able to use this knowledge in daily life is that most of us will try to appear small and narrow shouldered if we meet a group of big boys in a dark street. We look down and avoid taking up room in their minds. I believe that the reason for us not always being able to use the same method in educational work and care is that we associate the experience with anxiety, not control. As a matter of fact, we control the situation in the street with simple body language.

---

[*]   Blem 2007a, 2007b.

Sitting down

By sitting down, preferably on the floor, you take up less room in the service-user's mind. Furthermore, you tense fewer muscles in your body, and not the least the stomach. This means that the service-user will tense fewer muscles him- or herself, which lowers the level of adrenaline in the service-user and has a calming effect. Moreover, it is easier for you to calm down if you are sitting down instead of standing up.

Sometimes when I tell staff this, there is someone who says they would never dare to do so. They would risk being kicked in the head. I usually say that in that case they have sat down too late. You have to sit down when you feel the service-user is getting wound up.

Going down on one knee may be enough. Your muscles may not be as relaxed, but at least you take up less room in the service-user's mind.

Talking calmly

If the service-user loses control you should not speak at all. A boy I have worked with quite a lot says: 'It may be OK if they grab me, but they must shut up while doing so. Staff always have to speak so goddamn much.' Personally, I do not think it is OK to hold him the way he has been restrained, but I understand his frustration with babbling staff.

Before the service-user loses control, you may however get a good effect from talking. However, it is important to talk calmly and with a soothing tone. To scream or talk over-excitedly will probably only result in the service-user losing self-control. When talking calmly you can 'subtitle' or soothe.

Often the service-user does not understand what is going on. He or she may have been upset over another service-user having taken his or her coffee mug or seat. Very soon this may get out of perspective and the person loses self-control. To subtitle means that in this situation you say: 'It was hard for you that Peter took your mug. Should we ask him if you could have it back?' Then we do not only subtitle, but also give her hope of a possible solution.

You can soothe the service-user by talking calmly to him or her and thus help keep his or her focus. Some service-users wind themselves up, and then we can soothe them by being calm ourselves and talking to them about things we normally talk to them about. Do not talk about an ongoing conflict when you are going to soothe, but about daily life.

Giving in

I am aware that it sounds like defeat, but in a demand situation giving in is quite an effective way to avoid a conflict. To give in is simply an underestimated pedagogical method. All people afraid of conflicts know this. However, it is important not to give in the way people afraid of conflicts do, by saying 'If that is what you want then…' but to concede in a convincing way. We have already discussed this in chapter two where I suggested the principle 'It's never too late to give up'.

To concede in a good way is often about being good enough at making the correct demands so the service-user does not feel that the structure disappears when the member of staff gives in. This may, for example, be a plan to go for a long walk. The service-user does not want to. In that case the member of staff should say: 'Then let's go for a really short walk, just around the house.' The service-user does not lose but is able to meet the demand.

Sticking to a demand that the service-user is not ready for often results in an increase of level of affect. We straighten up and get ready for battle. We tense our muscles and even fasten our gaze on the service-user. If you concede in a demand situation, it is easier to use the methods described in the preceding pages.

To give in is not to give in every time a service-user wants something different from what we do; often it is about saving a situation. Afterwards you must relate to what happened in an educational or care framework. A familiar example:

Morgan is 14 years old. He has an intellectual disability and autism. His developmental age is about four years. Morgan is with his mother in the supermarket. They walk around with the shopping trolley. When the trolley is quite full they set out for the check-outs. Just before reaching the check-outs they pass the sweets shelves. Morgan wants a chocolate bar. His mother says no. Morgan screams and throws himself on the floor.

His mother takes the chocolate bar and puts it in the trolley. Morgan stops screaming and gets up. They pay for the groceries and Morgan has his chocolate bar.

Most people would think this was an awful solution. Morgan did not think so and the mother chose it herself. The solution would perhaps have been considered bad if Morgan had been an ordinary boy of four years of age. He is not. He is a boy with special needs. He would not learn much from not getting the chocolate bar. His mother's task for the next visit to the store, however, will be to prepare him for not getting a chocolate bar. This can be done in different ways, for example by agreeing on a reward if he will not scream in the supermarket, or by structure, or a social story. If he still is not able not to scream, then we should perhaps stop bringing him to the store. We should be careful about transferring ordinary fostering principles to the field of special needs. If they worked, you would never have taken the time to read this book.

Changing the staff

Not for infinity, but in the situation. Often affect is built up in the play between service-user and staff. To change one party means a hold-up of the build-up. The absolutely easiest solution is simply to make a change of staff. The new person enters the situation cool, calm and collected and immediately infects the service-user, even if he or she is in a state of chaos.

Leo is 31 years old. He has a severe degree of autism. Leo has no language and a long history of challenging behaviour. He lives in a group home where he always has two members of staff around him. Leo is a strong, big guy but his motor activity is fairly shaky.

When Leo hears an aeroplane but cannot see it for clouds he is anxious and often kicks the staff. The member of staff he gets at then exits the garden door and walks around in a 20-yard wide circle in the garden. Leo follows, but slowly because of his poor motor skill. All the time he is focused on the member of staff he is chasing. Then the member of staff enters the garden door and disappears into the hallway. Just inside the garden door the other member of staff is standing waiting for Leo. When Leo comes in he reaches out his hand and says: 'Hello, Leo.' Leo says politely hello and immediately lets go of his anxiety.

There can be different systems for changing staff. There can be a structure that says that every member of staff can always demand to be relieved when a situation is building up. You can also agree that every member of staff may ask another: 'Should I take over now?'

Parents can have the same kinds of agreement, but they may be harder to carry through in real life. If there are two parents, according to my experience, one of them is usually calmer than the other. Unfortunately this does not mean that it is always the calm person who takes over in chaotic situations. Sometimes as a parent you think that the other's method is not working properly, so you want to take over, even if you are not the calm one. It may be that neither of you is using methods that work properly and that neither trusts the other person's to. It must be somebody's fault and it is not mine! We have dealt with this at the beginning of the book in the section on giving blame. Don't! Agree with each other that when you feel a rise in frustration you relieve each other instead of building up a conflict.

If you are a single parent you unfortunately do not have the same possibilities. You can however choose to withdraw from a conflict, which may be just as good.

Using the 'snooker trick'

This expression was coined by my colleague Hanne Veje. Some service-users cannot manage any contact at all in a troubled situation; every contact results in chaos. They need to be left alone to be able to stay calm and keep self-control. In such cases you can talk to the person next to you about something soothing.

> **Peter** is anxious when he thinks it is time for food. He thinks it is about half an hour before lunch every day. The staff know this and they also know that in that half hour you cannot talk to Peter without him experiencing chaos. You can however talk to another service-user in the same room and say: 'How nice that we'll eat soon.' Then Peter stays calm.

Waiting

In many cases the service-user calms down if we simply wait him or her out without reacting. This is particularly true if the service-user's behaviour is strategy oriented, for example withdrawing or biting one's hand, but it may also work in a demand situation. The staff member makes a demand, the service-user reacts, but the reaction weakens if the staff member goes away for a while and waits. After a while the service-user is able to meet the demand. We cannot demand immediate realization of every demand or task without tensing our muscles. This may in many cases lead to a conflict.

All these methods aim to get the service-user to stay calm. This is accomplished by using methods that do not increase his or her intensity of affect. Consequently, we also limit the risk of being pulled into an increase of affect ourselves. We should make sure we are not infected by the service-user's anxiety and we should make sure to infect the service-user with our calm. We should be a calming factor in the service-user's life.

Creating diversions

In the 1960s quite some research was done in the US on diversion through absurd behaviour. The method is that when a service-user is anxious or starts to self-harm, the staff can solve the situation by, for example, jumping on one leg and making a noise like a rooster. Personally, I like the method because it makes a demand on the staff and not the service-user and because it came to us at a time when many methods in the field were all but humane. The method rose like a glowing torch in a dark time of horrendous numbers of assaults and institutionalized violence against service-users with intellectual disabilities, autism and mental illnesses. The researchers tried to find the optimal absurd behaviour by walking on their hands, screaming loudly or helping the service-user wreck furniture.

Some time in the 1970s, however, they realized that perhaps it was not the absurd behaviour that was central in the method, but the diversion. To make the service-user think of something other than what upset him or her. Therefore they started using different ways of diversion, for example by offering the service-user a cup of tea when he or she was anxious. It is, however, necessary to divert before the service-user has lost control. Diversion should in most cases be used in the very beginning of a build-up of affect. In my work I have found there are two main types of diversion – affective diversions and concrete diversions.

Affective diversions

Affective diversions are about using what we already know about affect to make the service-user gain control of him- or herself.

Humour is one way to create a diversion. As I have already discussed, the function of laughter is to release surplus affect. By making the service-user laugh, the affect is let go. You can make people laugh in different ways. A boy I have worked with for some time responds positively to the sentence 'And how d'you think things are?' Sometimes you can build up ways to make people laugh that are based on humour of repetition in this way.

At a conference I participated in, an American teacher, Michelle Garcia Winner, told us about what she calls the rubber chicken method. She bought a rubber chicken of the kind you give as a toy to dogs and keeps it on her desk in the classroom. When one of her pupils with autism is anxious, she uses it by saying: 'Now I think you need some rubber chicken' and touches the pupil's head with the chicken. In that situation the pupils cannot but laugh. The anxiety disappears at once. She has also bought small rubber chicken key rings for her pupils, which they bring to school and can squeeze if they get anxious. It is a clever way of using the cognitive method externalization in service-users with difficulties managing abstract concepts.

As staff or parents, you usually know how to make every individual service-user laugh. Use that knowledge in situations where the service-user is anxious to release the affect overload and the service-user can regain self-control.

Among other things it's a question of affect regulation and self-control. When you laugh you let go of harboured affect and you relax. And a relaxed person never fights. By helping the service-users to let go of affect we help them to calm down.

Another aspect of humour as a method of diversion is that it often helps create a trusting environment. We have previously looked at the importance of trust for the ability to keep self-control. To have a relationship with the service-user that is based on cordiality and trust means that the risk of incidents is small and that we can even be slightly sloppier with our methods; the service-user will manage our mistakes if he or she trusts the person who has messed up.

Another way of creating affective diversion is 'affect relief'. This is about creating possibilities for the service-user to feel the affect going away. This can be done in different ways:

> **Pierre** is 12 years old. He has autism and a level of function that corresponds to an age of 18 months. Pierre is a door-closer; he thinks that doors should be closed and that chairs should stand by tables, not be spread out in a room. He is often anxious and then starts to walk in circles, making loud noises and rubbing his eyes hard. After a while he often starts to hit himself hard in the face.
>
> When Pierre is anxious, a member of staff turns a chair over and walks a few metres away. When Pierre sees the chair he cannot not get up and raise the chair and put it in its place by the table. When he has done this he is clearly relieved and sighs loudly. The affect is gone and he is calm.

Some methods of physical diversion are based on this principle. The aim is to make the service-user release the affect and thereby regain self-control.

If you are in a dangerous situation where you are forced to use your right of self-defence it's safer to use physical diversion with affect relief than restraints. This method was worked out by a colleague of mine, Andy McDonnell, and may only be used when there is an immediate danger to the service-user or somebody else:

You grab the service-user's arms loosely and move them in circles in front of the body for five to eight seconds. Then you let go and immediately walk three metres away, preferably behind the service-user. At first the service-user is confused, but does not have the time to react until the member of staff has let go again. That the member of staff lets go, however, feels like a relief to the service-user, who therefore calms down at once in most cases. In rare cases the service-user continues his or her unsafe behaviour, in which case the procedure can be repeated. It is very rare that this has to be done more than a couple of times – most cases once is enough.

If the service-user hits herself in the head you can do a similar thing, but you must be careful not to hold the service-user's arms tight. Instead you should mirror her movements and with small pushes that prevent her hand coming into contact with her head. In most cases the service-user herself will move her arm in circles after a few seconds. Then you let go.

Once again it is about the service-user experiencing an affect relief; it simply feels good that the member of staff lets go. What is difficult in this situation is for the member of staff to let go; we have such difficulties letting go of physical control. It is, however, essential to be prepared to let go immediately if you are to grab a service-user at all. Otherwise you create a dangerous situation where there is a risk to both the service-user's and the staff member's safety.

Concrete diversions

Concrete diversions also work really well and are perhaps easier for most people to use. The aim of concrete diversions is to make the service-user think of something other than the build-up of affect. Concrete diversions should be considered alternatives to demands:

> **Uno** is 11 years old and has ADHD. He is often in conflict with his two-years-younger brother, Dio, who does not have any neuropsychiatric difficulties. Uno finds it incredibly hard to get out of conflicts and can often be in a conflict for hours. Dio, like all other boys his age, is interested in power and hierarchies and therefore challenges Uno's big brother status. Dio is about to surpass Uno in many areas, both in educational skills and general maturity, which contributes to the conflicts and Uno's frustration.
>
> When the boys have a conflict the parents usually make demands: 'Stop fighting, boys. Uno, go to your room, and Dio, go to yours!' This rarely has a particularly good effect, and most of the time the parents have to separate the boys by moving them away from each other.

One day the boys' mother instead says: 'How about we have some hot chocolate? Will you come out into the kitchen instead of lying there on the floor fighting?' The boys stop fighting and go to the kitchen where they sit down at opposite ends of the table, still slightly mad at each other, but they keep their calm.

Diversion was in this case more effective than the demand to stop fighting. It is even more effective in situations where a service-user winds herself up. By making the service-user think about something else she can cool down and regain full self-control.

Some service-users actively seek diversions:

Jasmin is six years old and has ADHD. She often winds herself up and is over-excited. In these situations it sometimes happens that she loses self-control and begins to bite or fight for no obvious reason. It starts with joy but ends in tears.

In situations where things are getting out of hand Jasmin has begun to ask her mother: 'Can't you tell me that we should go to sit down on the couch together soon, Mum?'

Jasmin really wants to be diverted but is not able to divert herself. By asking her mother to divert her, she manages to remain in control. She seeks outer affect regulation when the inner is not enough.

In my work, I have seen that you can change the method of working in educational settings or care by diverting actively and clearly. You can change things overnight so you divert instead of having to use physical restraint. However, it is hard work always to be diverting; you must concentrate and be alert all the time. You must get into the situation before it escalates.

Using the model of intensity of affect we looked at earlier in this chapter, you can see that you must act to divert after the trigger of the affect but before the service-user loses self-control (Figure 5.3). That period of time may be all from one second to several hours and is very individual. To work actively with diversion as the only method is therefore very hard. I have a little trick: with groups of staff who use a lot of restraints, I gave up years ago teaching them about working with structure and adjustment of demands. It is too abstract for them and they cannot see the connection between the

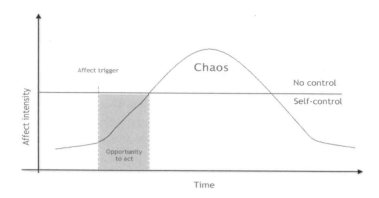

Figure 5.3 Between the affect trigger and loss of self-control – the opportunity to act to divert

daily methods and the restraints. So I teach them to divert. When I meet them again a month later I ask them how it is working. I always get the same response: 'It works well, we hardly use any restraints. What is hard is that you are always unbelievably tired when you get home from work; you must be on your toes all the time to be able to divert in time.' Then I can tell them about working with adjustment of demands and structure and they suddenly are able to see why it is good to work preventatively.

You should therefore consider diversion an emergency method that is preferably only one method of an arsenal of methods where the low-arousal approach, structure and preventative methods work together to focus on the self-control of the service-users.

Sometimes I hear people say: 'If you divert concretely there is a risk that you reward the negative behaviour.' We have already discussed that, but repetition may be good at times. I do not think that the risk is particularly great. If we could simply reward and thereby support negative behaviour, we could probably also easily reward and support positive behaviour, and then you probably would not need to take the time to read this book. There would be no point. If you are using rewards in the field of special education or care, you must do it very consciously by telling the person why the reward is given and at the same time make sure the reward is given immediately. That is not done when diverting. Nobody would think of saying: 'As you're fighting you'll get a cup of hot chocolate.' Besides, our service-users have difficulties generalizing one situation to another, which means that where they see a connection in one situation they will not necessarily understand that is also true in other similar situations.

You can divert concretely with edible things, for example ice cream, biscuits, sweets, food, soda, coffee, tea and the like, but you can also divert by activities, for example by reading a story, going for a walk or taking the car for a ride. However, most of the time such powerful means are not necessary. Making the service-user think of something else may be enough. You can say: 'Look, a bird' or ask a question where the service-user has to think before he or she can answer.

In some cases comforting diversions can be used:

Vince is ten years old and has a severe intellectual disability. He loves the nursery rhyme Incy Wincy Spider. If you hum Incy Wincy Spider when he is anxious he is immediately calm.

Vince is comforted by his favourite song and is relieved from the affect. He is lulled into peace and keeps his self-control so he can cooperate with us.

Confrontation or intervention?

By using the methods described in this chapter, both the low-arousal approach and diverting methods, you could have a daily life free of conflicts.* This means that we as staff have a better working environment, that occupational injuries are fewer and that we manage to work for many years with the same service-user. To parents it means an easier life to live and that their belief in the future increases. Furthermore, we get the bonus effect that children with neuropsychiatric disorders maintain trust in their parents and staff and therefore do not to the same degree seek acknowledgement

---

*   Pryor 2006.

outside the family in their youth. This means that the risk of them being assaulted or involved in criminality decreases a lot.

Some parents and staff, however, find it incredibly hard to think in a low-arousal way. They feel a loss of power and think that the people around them look at them as if they were crazy. In our society we have a blind faith in being tough and in consequential thinking, and in order to buy a child a chocolate bar to make him or her calm down by the sweets shelves in the store you must be sure of yourself as a parent.

The National Autistic Society sells a pin with the text 'I'm not naughty, I've got Autism' that the child can wear so other people can relate to their different behaviour and the perhaps different methods that are used in the field of special education and care. That is not a bad idea, but I think that those who suffer the most when other people are looking are the parents. As a parent you must dare believe in your methods, otherwise you will not carry them through. You must steel yourself and get out into the world with your children and believe that it is better to have a good day than to foster in a way that results in the child breaking.

A young man who one of my colleagues assessed was afraid to seem strange when other people said hello to him. Therefore he did not say hello back. People could stretch out their hand and he would not take it out of fear of seeming weird if he did not do it in the right way. By doing so he did something much stranger, which, however, he could not see himself. In the same way if a parent takes on a conflict about a chocolate bar with a crying and screaming 15-year-old in the supermarket, that will seem much stranger than if he or she gets his chocolate bar and we afterwards create a structure that helps us next time we are going to the store.

We should not win confrontations; we should create good interventions that lead to an increased quality of life for our service-users. We should create self-control instead of controlling.

Conflict-seeking service-users

If service-users actively seek conflicts to win, we must be careful not to be pulled in. You can still divert and use the low-arousal approach, which may have an effect, but it is much harder to stick to your methods when the service-user is confrontational. Conflict-seeking behaviour is often the result of many years of confrontations. The service-user is used to being in a confrontation and does not trust the world around her. Our task then is to increase the trust and create the possibility for cooperation. This is best done by being clear and straight in our communication with the service-user. We should say: 'I don't want to fight you, I want you to cooperate. I want you to decide for yourself, and I think that you'd like to cooperate if I treat you right.'

Many of our service-users are not used to straight-talking, nor do they understand euphemisms or the way we speak in order not to be confronting. To be straight and respectful often means that the service-user's trust increases. In a calm moment it is often also a good strategy to ask the service-user what he or she wants us to do if he or she is anxious. Service-users with neuropsychiatric disorders often have a clear idea of how they are best calmed. If we take that into consideration, we increase trust in the service-user and at the same time make our role as a supporting instead of controlling member of staff clear.

Some service-users want to be restrained because for many years they have been taught that it is the only way to calm down. They have learnt that they cannot take control themselves unless somebody else takes it first. This is a great problem if it is a service-user who moves freely in society.

Lennie is 16 years old. He has Tourette's syndrome and a long history of restraints. He has recently changed school and is now taking the bus to school. He has never done that before. The first day he takes the bus, he finds a good seat where he has a good view and therefore can see when he should push the stop button. He goes to school and has a good day and on his way home he sits in the same seat.

The following day Lennie enters the bus and sees that there is a man sitting in his seat. He says: 'That is my seat.' The man does not care, but says that there are no reserved seats in the bus. Lennie is angry and hits the man who begins to bleed from the nose. Other passengers enter the conflict and Lennie experiences a state of chaos and hits out violently for several minutes until the police arrive and hold him. Then Lennie is calm and thanks the police for helping him to calm down.

Next day his seat is available and he happily sits down. On the way home it is taken and he nicely asks a small elderly lady to move. She is afraid (Lennie is a big boy of 180 pounds and six feet) and moves.

The following day his seat is once again taken, He asks a young man to move. The man gives him the finger. Lennie calls to the driver: 'Call the police – I can't stop myself.' Then he hits the man hard in the head.'

Someone has taught Lennie that other people should take control of his life when he is anxious. Working with him at the new school no one held him even though he was lying on the floor screaming: 'Help me!' Eventually he learnt to take control himself. Now he can go by bus without help. If somebody is sitting in his seat, he nicely asks the person to move. If they say no, he does breathing exercises and decides whether he can control himself. If he can, he stays on the bus. If he cannot, he gets off and takes the next bus.

Summary

Conflicts occur when the service-user loses self-control. Often they happen when staff exhibit affect. A central concept in this area is affect contagion, where affects like anger, fear, anxiety or joy experienced by one person influence the people around her. People with intellectual disabilities or neuropsychiatric problems often have difficulties separating their own affects from others, thereby reacting to others' affects as if they were their own. Confrontative educational or care staff my therefore provoke service-users into a highly affective state, leaving them few possibilities of keeping self-control.

In order to keep the service-user calm, staff and parents need to stay calm themselves and use calming body language like keeping distance, avoiding eye contact or touch when the service-user is agitated. By using a neutral body language and a calm tone of voice, staff and parents can avoid violence, severe self-harm and a lot of anxiety in the service-user. The objective of the staff's and parents' behaviour in agitated situations must be to help the service-user maintain or regain self-control.

Chapter 6
• • • • • • •
Looking to the Future

The book you have almost finished by now has contained some principles for managing challenging behaviour. Some of the principles are fairly abstract and others are very concrete. In this final chapter I will bring together the most important of these. But I want to end the book with the hope that the future of special education and care will be free of the inhuman practices of the past.

Fundamental principles
People who can behave, will
This is a fundamental view of people that removes malicious motives, negative will and plenty of other devastating aspects from our relation with the service-user. If we start out from this principle, we can work giving respect to the service-user and move the responsibility of the care to ourselves. We cannot allow ourselves to leave the care to the service-user by talking about him or her as stubborn, unmotivated or malicious. If we think that the service-user should change, we must acknowledge that we cannot influence this very much. We only have the ability to exert an influence by changing the world around the service-user and our own way of meeting him or her. We must find out what it is the service-user is unable to do in situations where he or she has challenging behaviour, so we can change the conditions.

Ordinary fostering methods do not work on people with intellectual disabilities or neuropsychiatric disorders

We begin by using ordinary fostering methods. If they do not work, we often say 'There must be something wrong with the child' and refer him or her to a psychological or psychiatric assessment. If ordinary methods had worked, our service-users would never have been diagnosed. We must consequently find other methods.

Our methods must be founded on the service-user being in control

If we build our work on being in control over the service-user, we will have many conflicts and a negative development. If we acknowledge the service-user's strategies to keep self-control and actively support his or her efforts to stay in control, we can have a good daily life and the service-user can develop into being able to take care of him- or herself better without our constant assistance.

Our methods must aim at increasing the trust in us

If you are with someone you trust it is easier to keep your self-control. We must therefore watch out for signs that our methods reduce the service-user's trust. That may, for example, be that the service-user considers us unfair.

Make demands in a way that the service-user says yes

Everybody has the right to say no. We need to make the correct demand and make the demands so they are not unexpected. Use structure, and allow time to finish – and remember to give in when something clearly does not work.

Reduce the affect

Calm yourself down. Every time you feel you should take a step forwards you should take a step backwards. Then the service-user has a better chance of keeping self-control.

Divert – ice cream is better than conflicts

Remember to work with interventions instead of confrontations. Avoiding a conflict today means fewer conflicts to avoid tomorrow. Provoking a conflict today means you will have to be prepared for another one tomorrow. I would definitely choose the ice cream!

Leaving the past behind

For the last 20 years the world has witnessed a development in special educational and care activities nobody could have foreseen 50 years ago. Previously, methods believed to be necessary to create calm in care were used, even though the methods could be rough. We have discussed this earlier in the book.

In the last few years the focus has shifted. Today, society expects people in care to be treated well, no matter whether they are people with intellectual disabilities, neuropsychiatric disorders or simply elderly. Unfortunately, practice has not always kept up with changing attitudes and there have been scandals concerning the use of restraints and control holds in most European countries. Internationally, there have been several criminal convictions in cases where both care and therapeutic staff have committed assaults on service-users. These include, in most European countries, cases where service-users have not been seriously injured.

In the last 15 years, many incidents of abuse have become public thanks to the internet. Previously, you had to read all local newspapers to get a full picture; abuse of people with disabilities has never been considered news that would interest the public on a national level. Today there are a number of compilations of documented assaults, among others caica.org who have collected information on children who have died in educational or care settings.

The stories we now have broad access to thanks to the internet are cruel, horrible and terrifying. They have however made me realize that it is of utmost importance that we find ways of working other than those that have led to abuse. I hope that this book has helped by giving arguments and methods to work in a way that takes the service-users' difficulties, strengths and strategies into consideration.

We must create a special educational and care framework built on respect, care, rights and comfort.

This book is therefore dedicated to Christer Magnusson, 32 years old, who died in 2006 in Uppsala, Sweden, to Angellika Arndt, 7 years old, who died in 2006 in the US, and to all other people who have fallen victim to inhumane care methods.

References

[No authors listed.] (2006) 'Nurses monitor self-harm – UK trial.' *Australian Nurses Journal 13*, 10, 42. 1 May 2006.

Adewuya, A.O. and Famuyiwa, O.O. (2007) 'Attention deficit hyperactivity disorder among Nigerian primary school children: Prevalence and co-morbid conditions.' *European Child and Adolescent Psychiatry 16*, 1, 10–15.

Allik, H., Larsson, J.O. and Smedje, H. (2006) 'Insomnia in school-age children with Asperger syndrome or high-functioning autism.' *BMC Psychiatry 6*, 18.

Antonovsky, A. (1991) *Unraveling the Mystery of Health: How People Manage Stress and Stay Well.* Stockholm: Jossey-Bass.

Attwood, T. (2006) 'Asperger's Syndrome and Problems Related to Stress.' In M.G. Baron, J. Groden, G. Groden and L.P. Lipsitt (eds) *Stress and Coping in Autism.* Oxford: Oxford University Press.

Attwood, T. (2008) *The Complete Guide to Asperger's Syndrome.* London: Jessica Kingsley Publishers.

Bay, J. (2006) *Konsekvenspædagogik.* København: Borgen.

Blem, K.B. (2007a) Vold – Soldater på vagt. *Socialpædagogen* 2007–12.

Blem, K.B. (2007b) Vold – En vej til færre magtanvendelser. *Socialpædagogen* 2007–12.

Bowlby, J. (1973) *Attachment and Loss: Vol. 2. Separation: Anxiety and Anger.* London: Hogarth Press.

Bowlby, J. (1980) *Attachment and Loss: Vol. 3. Loss: Sadness and Depression.* London: Hogarth Press.

Bowlby, J. (1999) *Attachment and Loss: Vol. 1. Attachment* (2nd edn). New York, NY: Basic Books. (Original work published 1969)

Brøsen S.K. (2008) *Do You Understand Me?* London: Jessica Kingsley Publishers.

Caspi, A., McClay. J., Moffitt, T.E., Mill, J., Martin, J., Craig. I.W., Taylor, A. and Poulton, R. (2002) 'Role of genotype in the cycle of violence in maltreated children.' *Science 297*, 851–854.

Caspi, A. and Moffitt, T. (2006) 'Gene–environment interactions in psychiatry: Joining forces with neuroscience.' *Nature Reviews Neuroscience 7*, 583–590.

Cederblad, M. (1996) 'The children of the Lundby study as adults: A salutogenic perspective.' *European Child and Adolescent Psychiatry 5*, Suppl 1, 38–43.

Cernerud, L. (2004) 'Humour seen from a public health perspective.' *Scandinavian Journal of Public Health 5*, 396–398.

Claësson, B.H. and Idorn, U. (eds) (2005) *Holdingterapi: En familieterapeutisk metode til styrkelse af tilknytningen mellem børn og forældre.* Virum: Dansk Psykologisk Forlag.

Cooper, S.A., Smiley, E., Morrison, J., Allan, L., Williamson, A., Finlayson, J., Jackson, A. and Mantry, D. (2007) 'Psychosis and adults with intellectual disabilities: Prevalence, incidence, and related factors.' *Social Psychiatry and Psychiatric Epidemiology 42,* 7, 530–536.

Damasio, A.R. (1994) *Descartes' Error.* New York, NY: Putnam.

Darwin, C. (1998) *The Expression of Emotion in Man and Animals* (3rd edn). New York, NY: Oxford University Press. (Original work published 1867)

Deb, S., Clarke, D. and Unwin, G. (2006) *Using Medication to Manage Behaviour Problems among Adults with a Learning Disability: Quick Reference Guide.* Birmingham: University of Birmingham.

Detillion, C.E., Craft, T.K., Glasper, E.R., Prendergast, B.J. and DeVries, A.C. (2004) 'Social facilitation of wound healing.' *Psychoneuroendocrinology 29,* 8, 1004–1011.

Ditzen, B., Schmidt, S., Strauss, B., Nater, U.M., Ehlert, U. and Heinrichs, M. (2008) 'Adult attachment and social support interact to reduce psychological but not cortisol responses to stress.' *Journal of Psychosomatic Research 64,* 5, 479–486.

Ekman, P. (2003) *Emotions Revealed: Understanding Faces and Feelings.* London: Weidenfeld & Nicolson.

Emerson, E. (2001) *Challenging Behaviour* (2nd edn). Cambridge: Cambridge University Press.

Esbensen, A.J. and Benson, B.A. (2006) 'A prospective analysis of life events, problem behaviours and depression in adults with intellectual disability.' *Journal of Intellectual Disability Research 50,* 248–258.

Feldman, M.I. (ed.) (2002) *Sleisenger & Fordtran's Gastrointestinal and Liver Disease* (7th edn). Philadelphia, PA: WB Saunders.

Fisher, W.W., Bowman, L.G., Thompson, R.H. and Contrucci, S.A. (1998) 'Reductions in self injury reduced by transcutaneous electrical nerve stimulation.' *Journal of Applied Behavior Analysis 31,* 493–496.

Frank, E.D. (1983) 'Effects of parental disciplinary practices on characteristics of children: A review of the literature.' *The Southern Psychologist 1,* 2, 77–83.

Frith, U. (2003) *Autism: Explaining the Enigma* (2nd edn). Oxford: Blackwell.

Gershoff, E.T. (2002) 'Corporal punishment by parents and associated child behaviours and experiences: A meta-analytic and theoretical review.' *Psychological Bulletin 128,* 4, 539–579.

Ghaziuddin, M. (2005) *Mental Health Aspects of Autism and Asperger Syndrome.* London: Jessica Kingsley Publishers.

Ghaziuddin, M., Weidmer-Mikhail, E. and Ghaziuddin, N. (1998) 'Comorbidity of Asperger syndrome: A preliminary report.' *Journal of Intellectual Disability Research 42,* 4, 279–283.

Gneezy, U. and Rustichini, A. (2000) 'A Fine is a price.' *Journal of Legal Studies 29,* 1, 1–18.

Greenberg, J.S., Seltzer, M.M. and Hong, J. (2006) 'Bidirectional effects of expressed emotion and behaviour problems and symptoms in adolescents and adults with autism.' *American Journal of Mental Retardation 111,* 4, 229–249.

Greene, R.W. (1998) *The Explosive Child: A New Approach for Understanding and Parenting Easily Frustrated, Chronically Inflexible Children.* New York, NY: HarperCollins.

Groden, J., Baron, M.G. and Groden, G. (2006). 'Assessment and Coping Strategies.' In M.G. Baron, J. Groden, G. Groden and L.P. Lipsitt (eds) *Stress and Coping in Autism.* Oxford: Oxford University Press.

Hamilton, D., Sutherland, G. and Iacono, T. (2005) 'Further examination of relationships between life events and psychiatric symptoms in adults with intellectual disability.' *Journal of Intellectual Disability Research 49,* 839–844.

Hanley, G.P., Piazza, P.C., Keeney, K.M., Bakely-Smith, A.B. and Worsdell, A.F. (1998) 'Effects of wrist weights on self injurious and adaptive behaviors.' *Journal of Applied Behavior Analysis 31,* 307–310.

Harter, K. (2007, 12 March) 'Wisconsin clinic fined $100,000 in girl's death; employee gets 60 days jail.' *Pioneer Press Twin Cities.*

Hastings, R.P., Daley, D., Burns, C. and Beck, A. (2006) 'Maternal distress and expressed emotion: Cross-sectional and longitudinal relationships with behaviour problems of children with intellectual disabilities.' *American Journal of Mental Retardation 111,* 48–61.

Hejlskov Jørgensen, B., Jensen, L., Uhrskov, T., Bang-Neerup, T. and Prætorius, K. (2005) *Pubertet og løsrivelse.* Virum: Videnscenter for Autisme.

Hewett, D. (ed.) (1998) *Challenging Behaviour: Principles and Practices.* London: David Fulton.

Holmes, T.H. and Rahes, R.H. (1967) 'The social readjustment rating scale.' *Journal of Psychomatic Research 11,* 213–218.

Hurley, A.D., Folstein, M. and Lam, N. (2003) 'Patients with and without intellectual disability seeking outpatient psychiatric services: Diagnoses and prescribing pattern.' *Journal of Intellectual Disability Research 47,* 39–50.

Isen, A.M. and Levin, P.F. (1972) 'The effect of feeling good on helping: Cookies and kindness.' *Journal of Personality and Social Psychology 21,* 384–388.

James, W. (1884) 'What is an emotion?' *Mind 9,* 188–205.

Johansson, P., Hall, L., Gulz, A., Haake, M., Watanabe, K. (2007) 'Choice blindness and trust in the virtual world. Technical report of IEICE.' *HIP 107,* 60, 83–86.

Kadesjö, B. (2001) *Barn med koncentrationssvårigheter.* Stockholm: Liber.

Kanner, L. (1943) 'Autistic disturbances of affective contact.' *Nervous Child 2,* 217–250.

Kessler, R.C., Adler, L.A., Barkley, R. *et al.* (2006) 'The prevalence and correlates of adult ADHD in the United States: Results from the National Comorbidity Survey Replication.' *American Journal of Psychiatry 163,* 716–723.

Kiecolt-Glaser, J.K., Loving, T.J., Stowell, J.R. *et al.* (2005) 'Hostile marital interactions, proinflammatory cytokine production, and wound healing.' *Archives of Genetic Psychiatry 62,* 12, 1377–1384.

Kierkegaard, S. (1843) *Frygt og bæven.* København: Reitzel.

Kleibeuker, J.H. and Thijs, J.C. (2004) 'Functional dyspepsia.' *Current Opinion in Gastroenterology 20,* 6, 546–550.

Lam, D., Giles, A., and Lavander, A. (2003) 'Carers' expressed emotion, appraisal of behavioural problems and stress in children attending schools for learning disabilities.' *Journal of Intellectual Disability Research 47,* 456–463.

Langdon, P.E., Swift, A. and Budd, R. (2006) 'Social climate within secure inpatient services for people with intellectual disabilities.' *Journal of Intellectual Disability Research 50*, 828–836.

Lange, C.G. (1887) *Über Gemutsbewegungen.* Leipzig: no publisher listed.

LaVigna, G.W. and Willis, T.J. (2002) 'Counter-intuitive Strategies for Crisis Management Within a Non-aversive Framework.' In D. Allen (ed.) *Ethical Approaches to Physical Intervention.* Plymouth: BILD.

Lazarus, R. (1999) *Stress and Emotion: A New Synthesis.* New York, NY: Springer.

Linna, S.L., Moilanen, I., Ebeling, H., Piha, J., Kumpulainen, K., Tamminen, T. and Almqvist, F. (1999) 'Psychiatric symptoms in children with intellectual disability.' *European Journal of Child and Adolescent Psychiatry 8*, Suppl 4, 77–82.

Lueti, M., Meier, B. and Sandi, C. (2008) 'Stress effects on working memory, explicit memory, and implicit memory for neutral and emotional stimuli in healthy men.' *Frontal Behavioural Neuroscience 2*, 5.

Marucha, P.T., Kiecolt-Glaser, J.K. and Favagehi, M. (1998) 'Mucososal wound healing is impaired by examination stress.' *Psychosomatic Medicine 60*, 362–365.

Maughan, B. (1995) 'Annotation: Long-term outcomes of developmental reading problems.' *Journal of Child Psychology and Psychiatry 36*, 357–371.

McDonnell, A., Waters, T. and Jones, D. (2002) 'Low Arousal Approaches in the Management of Challenging Behaviours.' In D. Allen (ed.) *Ethical Approaches to Physical Intervention.* Plymouth: BILD.

McDonnell, A.A. (2010) *Managing Aggressive Behaviour in Care Settings: Understanding and Applying Low Arousal Approaches.* Chichester: Wiley-Blackwell.

Mercer, J., Sarner, L. and Rosa, L. (2006) 'Attachment Therapy on Trial: The Torture and Death of Candace Newmaker.' In G. Costa (ed.) *Child Psychology and Mental Health.* Westport, CT: Praeger Publishers.

Merrick, J. (2005) 'National survey 1998 on medical services for persons with intellectual disability in residential care in Israel.' *Journal of Endocrine Genetics 4*, 139–146.

Moffitt, T.E. (2005) 'The new look of behavioral genetics in developmental psychopathology: Gene–environment interplay in antisocial behaviors.' *Psychological Bulletin 131*, 4, 533–554.

Muris P., Steerneman, P., Merckelbach, H., Holdrinet, I. and Meesters, C. (1998) 'Comorbid anxiety symptoms in children with pervasive developmental disorders.' *Journal of Anxiety Disorders 12*, 4, 387–393.

Nathanson, D.L. (1992) *Shame and Pride: Affect, Sex, and the Birth of the Self.* New York, NY: W.W. Norton.

Nuechterlein, K.H. and Dawson, M.E. (1984) 'A heuristic vulnerability/stress model of schizophrenic episodes.' *Schizophrenia Bulletin 10*, 2, 300–312.

O'Farrell, T.J., Hooley, J., Fals-Stewart, W. and Cutter, H.S.G. (1998) 'Expressed emotion and relapse in alcoholic patients.' *Journal of Consulting and Clinical Psychology 66*, 744–752.

Paavonen, E.J., Nieminen-von Wendt, T., Vanhala, R., Aronen, E.T. and von Wendt,, L. (2003) 'Effectiveness of melatonin in the treatment of sleep disturbances in children with Asperger disorder.' *Journal of Child and Adolescent Pharmacology 13*, 1, 83–95.

Pinker, S. (2002) *The Blank Slate: The Modern Denial of Human Nature.* London: Allen Lane.

Pryor, J. (2006) 'What do nurses do in response to their predictions of aggression?' *Journal of Neuroscience Nursing 38*, 3, 177–182.

Revstedt, P. (2002) *Motivationsarbete* (3rd edn). Stockholm: Liber.

Rose, D. and Rose, J. (2005) 'Staff in services for people with intellectual disabilities: The impact of stress on attributions of challenging behaviour.' *Journal of Intellectual Disability Research 49*, 827–838.

Sandi, C. and Pinelo-Nava, M.T. (2007) 'Stress and memory: Behavioral effects and neurobiological mechanisms.' *Neural Plasticity*, 78970.

Schumacher, J., Hoffmann, P., Schmäl, C., Schulte-Körne, G. and Nöthen, M.M. (2007) 'Genetics of dyslexia: The evolving landscape.' *Journal of Medical Genetics 44*, 289–297.

Shalev, R.S., Manor, O., Kerem, B., Ayali, M., Badichi, N., Friedlander, Y. and Gross-Tsur, V. (2001) 'Developmental dyscalculia is a familial learning disability.' *Journal of Learning Disabilities 34*, 1, 59–65.

Sigsgaard, E. (2003) *Utskälld.* Stockholm: Liber.

Sigsgaard, E. (2007) *Skæld mindre ud.* København: Hans Reitzels Forlag.

Simoneau, T.L., Miklowitz, D.J. and Saleem, R. (1998) 'Expressed emotion and interactional patterns in the families of bipolar patients.' *Journal of Abnormal Psychology 107*, 497–507.

Sinkbæk, A. (2002) *Den romerske brobygger.* Bagsværd: Center for Autisme.

Skynner, R. and Cleese, J. (1993) *Families and How to Survive Them.* London: Random House.

Smiley, E. and Cooper, S.A. (2003) 'Intellectual disabilities, depressive episode, diagnostic criteria and diagnostic criteria for psychiatric disorders for use with adults with learning disabilities/mental retardation (DC-LD).' *Journal of Intellectual Disability Research 47*, 62–71.

Smolderen, K.G.E., Vingerhoets, A.J.J.M., Croon, M.A. and Denollet, J. (2007) 'Personality, psychological stress, and self-reported influenza symptomatology.' *BMC Public Health 7*, 339.

Solomon, R. and Serres, F. (1999) 'Effects of parental verbal aggression on children's self-esteem and school marks.' *Child Abuse and Neglect 23*, 4, 339–351.

Spreat, S., Conroy, J.W. and Jones, J.C. (1997) 'Use of psychotropic medication in Oklahoma: A statewide survey.' *American Journal of Mental Retardation 102*, 80–85.

Stern, D. (1985) *The Interpersonal World of the Infant: A View from Psychoanalysis and Development.* New York, NY: Basic Books.

Stern, D. (2004). *The Present Moment in Psychotherapy and Everyday Life.* New York, NY: W.W. Norton.

Stewart, M.E., Barnard, L., Pearson, J., Hasan, R. and O'Brien, G. (2006) 'Presentation of depression in autism and Asperger syndrome: A review.' *Autism 10*, 1, 103–116.

Sukhodolsky, D.G., Scahill, L., Gadow, K.D., *et al.* (2008) 'Parent-rated anxiety symptoms in children with pervasive developmental disorders: Frequency and association with core autism symptoms and cognitive functioning.' *Journal of Abnormal Child Psychology 3*, 1, 117–128.

Sung, V., Hiscock, H., Sciberras, E. and Efron, D. (2008) 'Sleep problems in children with attention-deficit/hyperactivity disorder: Prevalence and the effect on the child and family.' *Archives of Pediatric Adolescent Medicine 162*, 4, 336–342.

Tani, P., Lindberg, N., Nieminen-von Wendt, T., von Wendt, L., Alanko, L., Appelberg, B. and Porkka-Heiskanen, T. (2003) 'Insomnia is a frequent finding in adults with Asperger syndrome.' *BMC Psychiatry 3*, 12.

Tantam, D. (2003) 'The challenge of adolescents and adults with Asperger syndrome.' *Child and Adolescent Psychiatry Clinics of North America 12*, 143–163.

Tomkins, S.S. (1962) *Affect, Imagery, Consciousness. Vol I.* London: Tavistock.

Tomkins, S.S. (1963) *Affect, Imagery, Consciousness. Vol II, The Negative Affects.* New York, NY: Springer.

Tomkins, S.S. (1991) *Affect, Imagery, Consciousness. Vol III. The Negative Affects: Anger and Fear.* New York, NY: Springer.

Tosone, C. (2003) 'Living everyday lies: The experience of self.' *Clinical Social Work Journal 3*, 335–348.

Turk, J. (2003) 'Melatonin supplementation for severe and intractable sleep disturbance in young people with genetically determined developmental disabilities: Short review and commentary.' *Journal of Medical Genetics 40*, 11, 793–796.

Tsakanikos, E., Bouras, N., Costello, H. and Holt, G. (2007) 'Multiple exposure to life events and clinical psychopathology in adults with intellectual disability.' *Social Psychiatry and Psychiatric Epidemiology 42*, 24–28.

Turner, T.H. (1989) 'Schizophrenia and mental handicap: An historical review, with implications for further research.' *Psychological Medicine 19*, 301–314.

Uhrskov, T. and Hejlskov Jørgensen, B. (2007) 'Stress and Autism.' Paper presented at the conference Meeting of Minds II, Herning, Denmark.

van der Heijden, K.B., Smits, M.G., Van Someren, E.J., Ridderinkhof, K.R. and Gunning, W.B. (2007) 'Effect of melatonin on sleep, behavior, and cognition in ADHD and chronic sleep-onset insomnia.' *Journal of the American Academy of Child and Adolescent Psychiatry 46*, 2, 233–241.

van Duijvenvoorde, A.C.K., Zanolie, K., Rombouts, S.A.R.B., Raijmakers, M.E.J. and Crone, E.A. (2008) 'Evaluating the negative or valuing the positive? Neural mechanisms supporting feedback-based learning across development.' *Journal of Neuroscience 28*, 38, 9495–9503.

Wehmeyer, M.J. (2001) 'Self-determination and mental retardation.' *International Review of Research in Mental Retardation 24*, 1–41.

Weigel, L., Langdon, P.E., Collins, S. and O'Brien, Y. (2006) 'Challenging behaviour and learning disabilities: The relationship between expressed emotion and staff attributions.' *British Journal of Clinical Psychology 45*, 205–216.

Whitaker, P. (2001) *Challenging Behaviour and Autism.* London: National Autistic Society.

World Health Organization (1992) *International Classification of Diseases* (ICD-10). New York, NY: WHO.

Index

The introduction has not been indexed. Page locators in italics, represents information that can be found in tables or diagrams, etc. Footnotes *have* been indexed in this instance, as a high amount of information was contained within their entries (and are marked by an '*n*'.)